IDENTITY AND ADULTHOOD

Identity and Adulthood

EDITED BY
SUDHIR KAKAR

With an introductory lecture by
ERIK H. ERIKSON

DELHI
OXFORD UNIVERSITY PRESS
BOMBAY CALCUTTA MADRAS
1992

Oxford University Press, Walton Street, Oxford OX2 6DP

New York   Toronto
Delhi   Bombay   Calcutta   Madras   Karachi
Kuala Lumpur   Singapore   Hong Kong   Tokyo
Nairobi   Dar es Salaam
Melbourne   Auckland

and associates in
Berlin   Ibadan

First published 1979
Oxford India Paperbacks 1992

SBN 0 19 563159 5

Printed at Rekha Printers Pvt. Ltd., New Delhi 110020
and published by S. K. Mookerjee, Oxford University Press
YMCA Library Building, Jai Singh Road, New Delhi 110001

To the memory of
VIKRAM SARABHAI

CONTENTS

Preface   ix

I. THE HUMAN LIFE CYCLE

1   SETTING THE STAGE: The Traditional Hindu View
and the Psychology of Erik H. Erikson   3
By SUDHIR KAKAR

2   REPORT TO VIKRAM: Further Perspectives on the
Life Cycle   13
By ERIK H. ERIKSON

II. IDENTITY AND ADULTHOOD

3   TOWARD MATURITY: Problems of Identity seen in. the
Indian Clinical Setting   37
By B. K. RAMANUJAM

4   THE YOUNG AND THE OLD: Ambiguity of Role-models
and Values among Indian Youth   56
By DURGANAND SINHA

5   PASSAGE TO ADULTHOOD: Perceptions from Below   65
By S. K. THORAT

6   A Comment on 'Passage to Adulthood'   82
By SATISH SABERWAL

7   Reflections on the Social Construction of Adulthood   89
By VEENA DAS

8   SEARCH FOR AN IDENTITY: A Viewpoint of a Kannada
Writer   105
By U. R. ANANTHA MURTHY

9 RELATIVE REALITIES: Images of Adulthood in
Psychoanalysis and the Yogas   118
  By SUDHIR KAKAR

Notes on Contributors   131

Index   133

PREFACE

In January 1977, the Indian Council of Social Science Research held a month-long seminar on 'Identity and Adulthood'. Invited to lead the discussions and in fact the person around whose ideas this seminar was originally conceived and later organized, was Erik H. Erikson. Erikson's pioneer contributions to our understanding of the steps leading to adulthood provided us with the base from which we hoped to explore this terrain further in our own cultural setting.

Erikson, of course, is no stranger to India. On his first visit to India fifteen years ago, he gave a seminar in Ahmedabad on the human life cycle, and on his second visit a couple of years later, he spent many months in this country, while he worked on his book, *Gandhi's Truth*. This time, in addition to attending all our meetings, Erikson performed at our only public function, namely, the first Vikram Sarabhai Memorial Lecture of the I.C.S.S.R., which is reprinted here.

Now the term identity—and for that matter, as we increasingly realized, the concept of adulthood too—is so all-pervasive and is so much a part of the educated vocabulary that to pin down its precise meaning proves to be surprisingly difficult. From its origins in the clinical context, where a patient was described as having an identity disturbance when it was felt that there was a break in his sense of the self which prevented him from experiencing himself as a consistent and continuous being with a past, a present and a future, the meaning of the term identity has become quite varied. Its usage has expanded into so many different fields that the concept now seems to be more suggestive than rigorous, more evocative than abstractly definitive. 'Identity crisis' and the 'search for identity' are no longer confined to the individual but can characterize a group, an institution, a class, a profession, or even a nation.

Occasionally, one may even feel that the Upanishadic technique of knowing the *atman* by the reiteration of *neti* ('It is not this!') may lead to a better understanding of the identity concept than any intellectual attempts which aim to circumscribe its meaning. Thus the sense of identity is neither completely conscious nor unconscious, although at times it may appear to be exclusively the one or the other. It is not to be confused with the concepts of role or character although there may be a certain overlap in all three. It cannot be completely identified with such terms as self-conception and self-esteem, and a disturbance in the sense of identity is not the same as role conflict or a conflict in values, although occasionally it may be manifested as either. Perhaps we can come nearest to an understanding of the various dimensions of identity through a consideration of Erikson's clinical and theoretical contributions, as well as his biographical illustrations, which have clarified much without losing the necessary emotional charge so essential for any discussion of identity.

Erikson has given identity many meanings. For the purposes of our interdisciplinary seminar we could focus only on a couple. One of Erikson's major contributions to the notion of identity has been to show that the formation of individual identity, that sense of self-*sameness* and *continuity* in time and space, has as much to do with his group's basic way of organizing experience—his group identity—as with the vicissitudes of his personal development. The collective sense of identity characterizing the individual's significant social groups—his caste, class, nation or culture—gets transmitted to the infant's earliest bodily experience, entering the very core of his ego and thus becomes inextricably intertwined with his personal sense of identity which emerges from and is yet more than a sum of his earlier accrued identifications.

To give one of my favourite illustrations from Erikson's work on this interplay between the individual and the social: 'A child who has just found himself able to walk, for example, seems not only driven to repeat and perfect the act of walking by the promise of libidinal pleasure in the sense of Freud's locomotor eroticism, or by the need for mastery in the sense of Ivan Hendrick's work principle; he also becomes aware of the new status and stature of "one who can walk", with whatever connotation this happens to have in the co-ordinates of his culture's life plan—be it "one who will swiftly run after fleeing prey", "one who will go far", "one who will be upright", or "one who might go too far".' In discussing identity, personal growth and communal change cannot be separated; nor can we separate the identity crisis in individual development from the contemporary crisis in the historical development of his group (brought

about by technological or ideological developments and reorienta-
tions) since the two help to define each other and are truly relative to
each other. The term 'identity crisis' no longer carries the forebodings
of an impending pathological disaster but is 'accepted as designating
a necessary turning point, a crucial moment, when development must
move one way or another, marshalling resources of growth, recovery,
and further differentiation. This proves applicable to many situations: a crisis in individual development or the emergence of a new
élite, in the therapy of an individual or in the tensions of rapid
historical change.' It is precisely this location of identity in the core
of both the individual and his communal culture, its emergence from
the interplay of the psychological and the social, the developmental
and the historical, which makes the concept difficult to comprehend
and yet also gives it its power and promise for fruitful interdisciplinary work.

It is against this background of psycho-social relativity of the
concepts of identity and adulthood that we invited people from
different backgrounds and fields—history, psychology, psychiatry,
anthropology, sociology and literature—to engage in comparative
discussions of identity and adulthood as conceptualized in their
respective fields. We hoped, as Erikson put it in a letter, that, 'what
we really should *come* to discuss, wherever we start, is "Identity and
Generativity" within the individual life cycle, within the cycle of
generations in a given historical period and within the cycles of life
postulated by the dominant world image.' In practice, because of the
seminal nature of such interdisciplinary efforts, much of our discussion was confined to identity and adulthood in the Indian setting
today and we did not always succeed in putting the relativity of our
contributions at the centre of the discussion.

My first essay in this collection is the only one which was not
presented at the seminar. This early paper is included here because
it briefly presents, for those few who are not familiar with his work,
Erikson's theory of the human life cycle and compares it with the
classical Hindu *ashrama* scheme. In his own lecture, which he called
'Report to Vikram', Erikson enlarges on recent thoughts concerning
the human life cycle and especially adulthood, and illustrates the
comparative point of view by references to our seminar, including
our use of two films, the Swedish *Wild Strawberries*, and the Kannada *Samskara*.

Ramanujam presents rich case material illustrating some typical problems hindering the progress to adulthood in Indian urban society. Whereas the traditional social structure neither recognized adolescence as a distinct phase of the life cycle nor permitted the emergence of a cogent adult role, the transition from the traditional to the modern is bringing up many clinical problems such as those of emotional separation from the parents, the problems of identification with an 'absent' or distant father, the emotional dependence, the incapacity to make individual decisions and so on. He concludes his paper with observations on the ways early stages of life are handled in the Indian setting.

Sinha analyses the results of three empirical studies on intergenerational differences, which he carried out in a large north Indian city. As compared to the older generations, he finds the Indian youth of today characterized by a widespread ambiguity in values and an instability and uncertainty in the choice of role-models. Against the historical background of rapid social change and the migration of young students from rural areas to the cities, he feels that this role diffusion and value ambiguity has exacerbated the identity confusion of youth and is putting a strain on society's institutions which depend upon young people for their renewal.

Thorat gives us a vivid autobiographical account of an untouchable child's growing up in village India and his struggle against a demeaning, 'stigmatized' identity imposed by the dominant cultural and social groups. With the help of a secure base in the family and heady support from new ideological and social movements, Thorat describes his struggle to claim an adulthood which is otherwise denied to the oppressed. In his comment, Saberwal places this personal account in a broader, historical context. He describes the social and historical forces which converged during this period and gave a greater chance of success to this individual struggle against the 'stigmatized' identity.

The male and female life cycles among urban upper-caste Punjabis have been insightfully discussed by Veena Das. Drawing upon data from her fieldwork, popular fiction, and from sociological studies, she focuses on the contemporary meaning and realities of adulthood, for women and men, in this Punjabi community.

Anantha Murthy writes on the modern Indian writer's search for an identity. Influenced by western ideas and forms, admiring the 'insider's' knowledge of Indian traditions possessed by the older writers, yet rejecting their celebration of traditionalism and their aesthetic modes of expression, Anantha Murthy sensitively portrays the dilemmas of the creative writer in India's present historical situation, where the content, the form and the recipients of literature have all become 'problematic'.

In my concluding paper 'Relative Realities', I have compared and contrasted the notions of ideal adulthood in two 'therapeutic' systems—western psychoanalysis and the Hindu Yogic schools. Both these systems have transcended their original functions—cure of neuroses in the one and cure of spiritual malaise in the other. Both have strongly influenced the world views—the nature of man and the world he lives in—of their respective cultures. In this paper I have attempted to show that it is the different visions of reality underlying the two systems which have led to divergences in their ideals of psychological maturity.

We are grateful to the Indian Council of Social Science Research whose financial support made this seminar possible and especially to Mr J. P. Naik, for his unflagging interest and support. The contributions of Joan Erikson and Kamla Chowdhry were invaluable and we are most grateful. In conclusion, I wish to thank my wife Apeksha and my students Nimmi Parambi and Navnidhi Sakhlani for their help with the organization of the seminar and Satish Bahadur of the Film Institute for providing the visual material for discussion.

SUDHIR KAKAR

I. The Human Life Cycle

I

SETTING THE STAGE

The Traditional Hindu View and the Psychology of Erik H. Erikson*

SUDHIR KAKAR

Introduction

Recent developments in psychoanalysis, especially in its emphasis on 'ego strengths' (Heinz Hartmann) or 'basic virtues' (Erik Erikson), show a startling affinity to the Hindu *ashrama* (stages of life) theory. Though the phases of human development, like infancy, adolescence, etc. have been studied both by 'academic psychology' and by psychoanalysis, the study of the individual life cycle as a functional whole and as a 'link in the chain of generations' has been comparatively rare. Erikson has been the first psychoanalyst to treat this approach systematically.

Erikson sees human development not as a continuum, but as a series of predetermined steps or stages by which the individual seeks contact in an ever-widening radius with his society, which welcomes and regulates his 'unfolding'. Each phase of this development has a turning point, a crisis, which poses the solution of a specific task—a solution which is prepared in the preceding stages and is worked out further in the succeeding ones. The relative solution of each crisis in turn is the source of a specific psycho-social strength which is both the individual's heritage from and contribution to the succession of generations and to society's institutions. Erikson thus speaks of 'eight stages of man'.[1]

The *ashrama* theory, which was codified some two and a half thousand years ago in India by men like Manu and Gautama, also saw human development in terms of distinct stages of life, but at the

---

* This essay originally appeared in *Philosophy East and West*, 18(3), 1968.

same time considered the individual life cycle in its wholeness and in
the sequence of generations.

The aim of this paper is to see how far a 'factual' theory of the
human life cycle, based on clinical evidence and developed during
the last two decades in the West, corresponds to an 'ideal' theory
laid down in its essentials between the sixth and third centuries B.C.
in India.[2]

Methodological Considerations

To list the methodological considerations inherent in such a task
becomes a lament of the difficulties involved. First, the Hindu description of the 'stages of life' is articulated more in terms of 'what
should be' than of 'what is'. The Hindu view of psycho-social development, furthermore, though basing itself on the biological development of man, does not pay any attention to early childhood and to
the implications of today's theory of psycho-sexual stages (Freud's
oral, anal, and phallic phases), although it must be said that the rites
which accompany the child's early development indicate a definite
awareness of some critical stages. The Hindu view proposes 'ideal'
images in Plato's sense and thus permits a comparison only between
the personal requirements implicit in the prescribed duties of each
stage of the Hindu life cycle and Erikson's 'virtues'.[3]

The second difficulty lies in grasping the original meaning of basic
Hindu concepts such as *dharma*, *moksha*, etc., since the meanings of
these concepts have changed, if ever so subtly, during the last two
and a half thousand years. This difficulty is of course inherent in any
history of ideas where the meaning of insightful concepts in a particular time in history has again to be recaptured in a different period.

Basic Assumptions of the Two Systems

The basic concept underlying the Hindu view is that of *dharma*.
First mentioned in the *Rigveda*, the concept has passed through many
vicissitudes. The list of formal treatises on *dharma*, starting from
Gautama's *Dharmashastra* (*c.* 600 B.C.?) to the present day, covers
172 pages in Kane's *History of Dharmashastra*.[4] At the present time,
dharma is variously translated as 'law', 'moral duty', 'right action',
or 'conformity with the truth of things'.[5] For our purpose *dharma* has
two implications—individual and social.

From the individual's point of view *dharma* is the ground plan of
his life which will lead to self-realization. An individual's *dharma* is

thus his ideal life cycle. According to the *Vaisesikasutra*, it is 'that from which results happiness and final beatitude'.[6] If a person is then known by his *dharma*, the question arises, how can he know of it, that is, know what his ideal life cycle is? How are his actions to be judged as being or not being in conformity with *dharma*? Though a person is enjoined to base his actions on the precepts of the Dharma-shastras, on the lives of men who have attained self-realization, and on his own understanding, the final answer is that no one can really, in any absolute sense, know what his *dharma* is. This is due to the fact that a man's *dharma* is always considered with regard to four factors: (1) *desha* (country, region), which I would call the culture to which he belongs; (2) *kala* (time), the period of history in which he lives; (3) *shrama* (work), which takes into account his stage of life; and (4) *guna* (attribute), which refers to what Prabhu calls the inherent psycho-biological traits.[7] The meaning of a man's action can be derived only out of a consideration of these four factors. This, then, is the Hindu methodology which leads to the first comparison —a methodological one—with the psychoanalytical, 'genetic' approach.

Erikson has also stressed the fact that for a 'meaning' to be extracted out of an event in an individual's life (dream, association, action), it has to be studied with regard to what can be termed four 'coordinates': (1) the contemporary stage of life of the individual; (2) his life history (psycho-sexual and psycho-social); (3) the contemporary stage of the socio-cultural unit of which he is a part; and (4) the history of the socio-cultural unit.[8]

The similarities with the Hindu approach are immediately evident. The first coordinate in the clinical methodology is the Hindu *shrama*, the third one is *desha*, and the fourth, *kala*. The only difference lies in the second coordinate. Whereas Erikson's approach, and that of western science since Freud, treat infantile development as the adult's pre-history, the doctrine of the *gunas*, in line with the belief in rebirth, considered human development to be anchored in a succession of previous lives. An individual is thus born a Brahmin and does not become one.

The second implication, a social one, of the concept of *dharma* is the crucial assumption in Hindu theory of the life cycle and stages of life (*ashrama-dharma*). As a social force, some modern authors define it as the 'process and instrument of integration' that underlies all modes of association'.[9] It is the 'mechanism of social interaction'.[10]

The word itself is derived from the root *dhṛ* (to uphold, to support, to nourish) and in a few passages of the *Rigveda* it appears to be used in the sense of upholder or sustainer. In its social implication, *dharma* is an inherent force in human beings which holds the individual and the society together, or, going one step further, the force which makes the individual and the society hold each other together. It is synonymous with the basic assumption of Erikson's theory, 'mutuality', that is, '(a) a growing person's readiness to interact with a widening social radius in predetermined steps, and (b) the readiness of society to welcome, invite, and influence this interaction'.[11] It is this mutuality which is the 'maintenance of the human world',[12] and this is also the Hindu view as expressed in the *Mahabharata:* 'Neither the state nor the king, neither the mace nor the mace-bearer, govern the people; it is only by *dharma* that people secure mutual protection.'[13]

The Stages of Life and Ashramadharma

Infancy, the first stage in Erikson's model, has the task of resolving the first crisis, namely, 'basic trust' v. 'mistrust'.[14] The successful resolution depends on the mutuality between the mother and the infant, so that the mother represents an almost somatic conviction to the child that both she and he are 'trustworthy'. A successful resolution, that is, a favourable ratio of basic trust over mistrust, gives the developing individual the ontogenic basis of the first and the basic virtue: 'hope'.

Early childhood, the second stage, is marked by increasing muscular and locomotor coordination as well as maturing cognitive discrimination. The child's will comes up against parental will and the task of this stage is a favourable resolution of 'autonomy' v. 'shame, doubt', and the basis for the second virtue: 'will power'.

In the third, the play stage, the child is able to move about more independently, guided by the beginnings of a conscience and a dawning comprehension of his expected role in the adult world. Competition with age-mates in play and with the father in phantasy makes him aware of his inferior equipment, and the task for this stage lies in the favourable resolution of 'initiative' v. 'guilt' and the issuing virtue of 'purposefulness'.

The Hindu authors of the *ashrama* theory did not consider the first three stages either in their psycho-sexual or in their psycho-social implications. Since they developed the stages of life from a social viewpoint, it was their opinion that the *upanayana* ceremony, performed sometime between the ages of five and ten, was the real dividing line between the individual-individual and the social-individual. Daksha's opinion is shared by many authors: 'Till a boy is eight years old he is like one newly born and only indicates the caste in which he is born. As long as his *upanayana* ceremony is not performed the boy incurs no blame as to what is allowed or forbidden.'[15] The rituals of *jatakarman*, *annaprasana*, and *caula*, roughly coinciding with the beginnings of the first three Eriksonian stages, indicate a certain awareness of the turning points in the first three years of life. 'Hope', which Erikson has called the basic virtue and which is attributed to the first stage of life (while a weakness in basic hope.disposes the individual to severe mental regression), was in the Hindu view equally basic, but attributable to the creation of human life itself and thus transcending any individual time–space continuum. This is seen in the following excerpt from the *Mahabharata*:

Whence, however, does Hope arise? . . . Hope is the sheet-anchor of every man. When that Hope is destroyed, great grief follows which, forsooth, is almost equal to death itself. . . . I think that Hope is bigger than a mountain with all its trees. Or, perhaps, it is bigger than the sky itself. Or, perhaps, O King, it is really immeasurable. Hope, O Chief of *kurus*, is highly difficult of being understood and equally difficult of being conquered. Seeing this last attribute of Hope, I ask, what else is so unconquerable as this?[16]

The fourth stage in Erikson's theory is that of the 'birth into the community' obligatory in the school age, where the child begins to learn the skills and to become acquainted with the tool world of his culture in preparation for his adult role as a provider. The task of this stage then lies in 'industry' v. 'inferiority', and the emerging strength is 'competence'.

The following stage is that of adolescence, where the overriding concern is with winning an identity, that is, '. . . the accrued confidence that the inner sameness and continuity prepared in the past are matched by the sameness and continuity of one's meaning for others, as evidenced in the tangible promise of a "career".'[17] The strength issuing from a favourable ratio of 'identity' v. 'identity confusion' is 'fidelity', which permits the youth to be true to himself and to 'significant others', including systems of belief.

These last two stages obviously correspond to the two parts of the first *ashrama* of the Hindu theory, that of *brahmacharya*, in which the school child, growing into youth, learned the basic skills relevant to his future adult working role while he lived together with other students and the guru. The myriad duties prescribed for this stage can be subsumed under two headings: (a) the social importance placed on the learning of skills, and (b) the student's unquestioning devotion to the guru's person. The task in the *brahmacharya* stage, I would say, lies in the knowing of one's *dharma*, which would consist in acquiring the skills in one's caste and in winning an identity based on a caste identity and the identification with and the emulation of the guru. The strengths issuing from this stage would then correspond to 'competence' and 'fidelity'. The difference again lies in the fact that whereas in the Eriksonian model identity is based on psycho-social development dependent on one life cycle, in the Hindu view it would be a result of the *gunas* and thus based on psycho-social fate through many life cycles.

The next stage in Erikson's scheme is that of young adulthood, in which the person who has consolidated his identity is ready for 'intimacy' with another. The task in this stage lies in the resolution of the conflict between 'intimacy' and 'isolation', and the resulting strength is mature 'love'. By 'love' Erikson means not only the mutuality of shared eroticism and trust but also a shared regulation of the cycles of work, procreation, and recreation.[18]

This stage would then correspond to the early part of *garhasthya*, the second stage of the *ashrama* theory. In the Hindu view it is in this stage that 'man's-meanings' (*purusarthas*) besides *dharma*, i.e. *artha* (material gratification) and *kama* (sensual-sexual gratification), flower and are to be enjoyed. The Hindu view thus also hints at the 'intimacy' based on shared work as well as on sensuality and procreation. 'He only is a perfect man who consists of three persons united, his wife, himself, and his offspring.'[19]

The next Erikson stage is that of adulthood, when the primary concern becomes that of generativity, of establishing and guiding the next generation and of producing the means of maintaining the social world. The crisis in this stage is that of 'generativity' v. 'stagnation' and the ensuing strength, 'care', which Erikson calls the widening concern for what has been generated by love and productivity.

This stage corresponds to the later part of *garhasthya*, and the third *ashrama* of *vanaprastha* (a gradual withdrawal without a loosening of responsibility). In his book *Childhood and Society*, Erikson has the following to say about the stage of adulthood and its concern with generativity: 'In this book the emphasis is on the childhood stages, otherwise the section on generativity would be of necessity a central one, for this term encompasses the evolutionary development which has made man the teaching and instituting as well as the learning animal.'[20] The importance placed on generativity is shared by Hindu writers. 'And in accordance with the precepts of the *Veda* and of the *Smriti*, the housekeeper is declared to be superior to all of them; for he supports the other three. As all rivers, both great and small, find a resting-place in the ocean, even so men of all orders find protection with householders.'[21] Yet in the Hindu view the later part of the *garhasthya* stage and the *vanaprastha* both deal with generativity and care, one in the narrow sense and the other in a widened sense. This is the reason why the two stages were not separated by some Hindu writers. The difference is that whereas the care in the first case was limited to one's own immediate family (insofar as that care can be so limited), *vanaprastha* was followed by an inner withdrawal from family affairs and family ties. The individuals, now being consulted by the community, practised a widened concept of generativity. The care thus extended from one's own family to the community at large; a man's interest turned from the sphere of the family to the sphere of public affairs. In attempting to separate the two, one may well see the primary task of the householder in the practice of *dharma*, and the primary task of the *vanaprasthin* in the teaching of *dharma*. Although the life-span from the beginning of young adulthood to the end of adulthood in Erikson's model would correspond to a similar span from the beginning of *garhasthya* to the end of *vanaprastha*, the dividing line between the two stages differs in the two models. But this again may well have to do with a difference in the total images of the life cycle: in the Hindu view the separation from what holds one to 'this life' only prepares a rebirth into another section of life on earth.

The last stage in Erikson's scheme is that of old age, with its crisis of 'integrity' v. 'despair' and the strength of 'wisdom'. Integrity means the emotional and cognitive integrity accruing from the preceding stages in spite of the decline of bodily and mental functions. It is '. . . the acceptance of one's one and only life cycle as something that had to be and that by necessity permitted of no substitutions'.[22] The ancient Hindu writers would completely agree with Erikson's statement if the words 'and only' were omitted. For, in Hindu terms, integrity is the acceptance of one's *svadharma*, and they are aware of its counterpart, despair. 'Better one's own *dharma*, bereft of merit, than another's well-performed; the death in one's own *dharma* is praise-worthy, the living in another's is fearsome' (*Bhagavadgita* III. 35).

The last stage of Erikson's model corresponds with the *samnyasa* (renunciation), showing the same concern with self-realization (*moksha*). The difference is that the Hindu view demands the physical separation of the individual from all worldly and personal ties. 'Inner emigration' is not enough. The 'indifference' or detachment is in the realization of *svadharma*, the task for this stage, and leading to the Hindu concept of wisdom. Renunciation, however, according to the *Gita*, does not pertain to all action, but only to selfish actions and the fruits of all action; it is the surrender of the notions of I and Mine.

Conclusion

From the above it appears that there is a suggestive convergence (though, of course, not an absolute correspondence) of the image of the human life cycle as expounded by the unknown, or at least mythical, builders of *ashrama-dharma* and the modern theory of Erik Erikson. Both schemes see human development in terms of stages of life, each of which contributes a specific strength, with the strengths (and the stages) integrated into a functional whole, the object of which is self-realization and transcendence. In both theories, the individual at any stage of life is not viewed in isolation, but in inter-action with the sequence of generations and in shared mutuality. There are three fundamental differences. First of all, the Hindu view is a religious or 'ideal' one while Erikson's approach is clinical and developmental. Thus Erikson sees each stage not only as a turning point but also as a crisis, which can 'turn out badly', i.e. lead to specific pathological syndromes. Secondly, the Hindu theory gives a certain importance to a combination of traits (*gunas*) from previous lives in considering the psycho-social development of the individual. And finally, the Hindu theory ignores Erikson's first three stages as well as infantile sexuality, insights which we owe to the break-through of modern psychology into man's individual pre-history.

Yet it is not the convergence which is so remarkable, since both the religious endeavour to give meaning to the stages of life, and the scholar's attempt to correlate the attributes of these stages must be based on what evolution has created: human growth and develop-ment. What is more astonishing is the scarcity of attempts to com-prehend the human life cycle in its stages as well as in its totality, either in religious or developmental literature, or indeed in poetry,

ERIKSON'S SCHEME		HINDU SCHEME	
STAGE	SPECIFIC TASK AND 'VIRTUE'	STAGE	SPECIFIC TASK AND 'VIRTUE'
1. Infancy	Basic Trust v. Mistrust: Hope	Individual's pre-history—not explicitly considered	Preparation of the capacity to comprehend *dharma*
2. Early Childhood	Autonomy v. Shame, Doubt: Will-power		
3. Play Age	Initiative v. Guilt: Purposefulness		
4. School Age	Industry v. Inferiority: Competence	1. Apprenticeship (*brahmacharya*)	Knowledge of *dharma*: Competence and Fidelity
5. Adolescence	Identity v. Identity Confusion: Fidelity		
6. Young Adulthood	Intimacy v. Isolation: Love	2. Householder (*garhasthya*)	Practice of *dharma*: Love and Care
7. Adulthood	Generativity v. Stagnation: Care	3. Withdrawal (*vanaprastha*)	Teaching of *dharma*: Extended Care
8. Old Age	Integrity v. Despair: Wisdom	4. Renunciation (*sannyasa*)	Realization of *dharma*: Wisdom

Shakespeare's fascination with the 'seven ages of man' notwithstanding.[23]

The chart on page 11 attempts to summarize the two views that have been discussed.

NOTES AND REFERENCES

1. Erik Erikson, 'Eight Ages of Man', in *Childhood and Society*, New York, W. W. Norton and Co., 1963. See further, 'Human Strength and the Cycle of Generations', in *Insight and Responsibility*, New York, W. W. Norton and Co., 1964.
2. Though the Hindu stages of life were known in Vedic times and are clearly mentioned in the *Upanishads*, e.g. in the *Chandogyopanishad*, a detailed account of the duties and rights of each stage is given in the various *Dharmashastras* of which *Manusmriti* (*c.* 600–300 B.C.) and *Yajnavalkyasmriti* (*c.* 100 B.C.–A.D. 300) are the more important ones. See P. V. Kane, *History of Dharmasastra*, Poona, Bhandarkar-Oriental Research Institute, 1933, vol. 1, Part 1, pp. 12–20 and vol. 2, Part 1, pp. 416–26.
3. Erikson, *Childhood and Society*, p. 274.
4. Kane, op. cit., vol. 1, Part 1, pp. 507–678.
5. S. Radhakrishnan, *The Hindu View of Life*, London, George Allen & Unwin Ltd., 1927, pp. 77–8.
6. Kane, op. cit., vol. 1, Part 1, p. 3.
7. P. N. Prabhu, *Hindu Social Organisation*, Bombay, Popular Book Depot, 1954, p. 73.
8. Erikson's methodological approach comes through clearly in 'The Nature of Clinical Evidence', in *Insight and Responsibility*, and 'Relevance and Relativity in Case History', in *Childhood and Society*.
9. K. Motwani, *Manu Dharma Sastra*, Madras, Ganesh & Co., 1958, p. 24.
10. Ibid., p. 377.
11. Erikson, *Childhood and Society*, p. 270.
12. Ibid., p. 270.
13. Cited in Prabhu, op. cit., p. 73.
14. Because of space considerations, Erikson's theory is presented in an extremely abbreviated form.
15. Kane, op. cit., vol. 2, Part 1, p. 188.
16. *Mahabharata* (Santiparva), M. N. Dutt, trans., Calcutta, R. M. Sircar, 1902, p. 186.
17. Erikson, *Childhood and Society*, p. 264.
18. Ibid., p. 266.
19. *The Laws of Manu*, G. Buhler, trans., *Sacred Books of the East*, vol. XXV, Oxford, Clarendon Press, 1886, p. 335.
20. Erikson, *Childhood and Society*, p. 266.
21. *The Laws of Manu*, pp. 214–15.
22. Erikson, *Childhood and Society*, p. 268.
23. Shakespeare, *As You Like It*, II. vii.

2

REPORT TO VIKRAM

Further Perspectives on the Life Cycle

ERIK H. ERIKSON

1

I can best evoke Vikram Sarabhai's personality and manifold interests by recalling where I saw him first and last, and where we worked together most concentratedly. It was on our first visit to India in 1962 that Vikram met us in Delhi and immediately, while the time of year still permitted, took us to Srinagar and up to the Solar Ray Laboratory in Gulmarg. That year of the Chinese invasion those deep and pensive valleys resounded with the droning of warplanes. And I saw Vikram last a decade later on the island of Delos in the Aegean Sea where he presided at a ceremony which concluded one of the yearly conferences convoked by the late architect Doxiades: on that cruise we had discussed the rights of children and youths to developmental space, as it were, in the city of the future. In between these two meetings, he invited me, while I was in India, to attend a Pugwash Conference in the island palace of Udaipur where a number of nationalities cautiously faced each other in order to discuss the dangers and promises of nuclear power.

For me, who thus witnessed Vikram Sarabhai's far-flung interests, all close to politics in the widest sense, and who was aware also of his systematic and experimental mind, it is a moving memory to have been most intimately associated with him in the early sixties in his home town of Ahmedabad in a seminar on the stages of human life. Through this interdisciplinary seminar—planned by Kamla

First Vikram Sarabhai Memorial Lecture of the ICSSR, delivered on 9 February 1977 in New Delhi. Manuscript revised and completed with the support of a grant from the Maurice Falk Foundation to the Mt Zion Hospital in San Francisco.

Chowdhry for the Indian Institute of Management—I met Vikram's astounding family. The B. M. Institute, founded by Vikram's brother Gautam and led by Kamalini Sarabhai, provided, of course, professional support to our proceedings; while Mrinalini Sarabhai staged a finale for our meetings on the grounds of their house by the Sabarmati, where she and her group of dancers performed themes from the Hindu life cycle.

Now, fifteen years later, I am here in Delhi for another seminar on 'Identity and Adulthood in India'. Vikram is not among us. But I propose to testify to his pervasive presence by reporting to him, as it were, on the directions which our thinking has pursued since we first discussed the human life cycle in Ahmedabad. Our theory, as submitted then, has, in the meantime, been formulated and compared with the traditional Hindu point of view in a comprehensive essay by Sudhir Kakar. But I will have to repeat, somewhat didactically, some of its fundamental assumptions as I attempt to advance from the insights of the 'century of the child' to those of the (sometimes shocking) decades of youth, to our present concerns with adulthood in different modern contexts. But of course, even such systematic progression must always begin with the interplay of childhood, youth and adulthood, both in the individual life cycle and in the cycle of generations. And in this context I recall Vikram Sarabhai's very countenance as significant for our discourse. For the characteristic of his facial expression which I remember most vividly is the naturalness with which he could shift from childlike laughter to deep and sometimes melancholy concern, and back. (I dare to add only in parenthesis that he reminded me, on such occasions, of the double image of Krishna as adviser and interpreter to the powerful and as the radiant boy child disarming all the world with his smile.) But Vikram, in some ways, not only personified, he also had a rare understanding of, the relationship of childhood and adulthood, a relationship which, it seems, must be reformulated from age to age. In this regard I could quote—and, in fact, have done so in my last book, *Toys and Reasons*—Vikram's great colleague Albert Einstein, who was uniquely aware of the child in himself. For while in his childhood proper he was avidly and earnestly active with building blocks and jigsaw puzzles—being slower than most in learning to speak—he later, as a famous scientist, expressed the 'psychological viewpoint' that 'combinatory play seems to be the essential feature in productive thought—before there is any connection with logical construction in words or other kinds of signs which can be communicated to others'.[1]

Here, as in other references to the playfulness acquired in childhood, he does not speak of it as an immature preparation for adulthood but as an essential feature that matures throughout life, finding ever 'higher' manifestations.

2

It is this holistic approach which I would like to pursue today as I first discuss the intricate importance of each stage of life to all and that of all to each, and then enlarge on the relationship of each and all stages to the basic structure of human society. This, of course, is not news to the students of the Hindu division of life into *ashramas* which are essential parts of a preordained *dharma*. But there seem to be significant omissions in every account of human life as a whole. The Hindu system neglects to assign any formal importance to the stages of childhood. One may, then, well begin, as Freud was forced to do, with the question of what is omitted or even repressed in the overall imagery of the course of life—and in what way does, to use a psychoanalytic term, the 'repressed return'? I should first admit, however, that we of the psychoanalytic establishment are forced to recognize today that in our 'originological' emphasis on the newly discovered childhood stages (and especially those of infantile sexuality) we, in turn, have come to pay too little attention to the structure and function of later stages, and especially of adulthood, in their own right. In such matters, changing emphases seem to lead to new oversights.

As to Shakespeare's famous list of seven ages in *As You Like It*, the very title of the play forbids us to make too much of it, and too seriously. But is it not strange that this playwright mentions no play age, this passionate genius no stage of adolescence, this creator no stage of parenthood? Instead, he depicts on all the world's stage, seven acts: the 'mewling and puking' infant, the 'whining school-boy' 'creeping like snail unwillingly to school', and then, 'the lover', the 'soldier', and 'the justice', followed by two rapidly declining oldsters, one marked by 'childish treble' and the other, by 'second childishness'. Where is the first, the original, childhood between babyhood and school age?

The answer may be that both Shakespeare and the Hindu scriptures—where the first 'real' stage of life is that of apprenticeship—

seem to concentrate on explicitly male categorizations. Even Shakespeare's infant, it is true, has a nurse (which may not be holding it
too tenderly), but otherwise those early years when women have, so
far, been the arbiters of intense and (as we now know) decisive
developments, are, in male accounts, apt to be treated as a kind of
opaque pre-history.

Now, we know that the Hindu rites and folkways dealing with
childhood stages and the myths and fairy tales dramatizing them
betray an intimate, implicit understanding of the fatefulness of early
life. Furthermore, the Hindu scriptures, in their elaboration of four
major dimensions of human fate, seem to 'know' every aspect of the
complex psycho-bio-social unity of life which the modern disciplines
dealing with man can only demonstrate cooperatively. If I may
translate these dimensions into my own terms: *desha*, the socio-
cultural setting in which we grow up, and *kala*, the past and present
history of that setting; *shrama*, the stage of life within the life
assigned to us within the cycle of rebirths, and *guna*, our resulting
personal makeup. But, of course, this outline projects on a grandiose
metaphysical Happening much of what today we would, at least in
my field, try to ascribe to the psycho-social conditions of individual
childhood and to the evolution of the species.

And here we can recognize as an important 'psycho-historical'
principle the (already mentioned) fact that in any given world images
the ontogenetic and the phylogenetic past are apt to fuse into one
mythic pre-history. Thus, the Hindu life spiral combines *dharma*, the
law of the present life, with *karma*, the net balance of good and bad
deeds in previous lives, and defines a person's identity as well as his
adult goals as aspects of one inescapable truth which unifies rather
than contrasts our earthly and our existential identities.

Faced with a traditional world image of such consistency and
persuasiveness as the Hindu world, however, we, observers and
diagnosticians of today, cannot ignore or simply leave behind some
fundamental questions in the comparative observation of life histories. One such question is that of the residual power, even under
conditions of rapid modernization, of the traditional world images
which are based on ancient religions: how can we study their continued presence and viability in ourselves and in our subjects,
whether our methodology is that of individual or of social psychology
and whether or not it includes a systematic concern with unconscious
motivation? And just when we may be inclined to declare as obsolete

in ourselves and in those around us the last versions of a universal world image that we and our forebears have grown up with, are we not obliged to ask what gaping lesions are left in man's total orientation when these ancient world images are fragmented? And what substitutes—belief systems, ideologies, theories—are undertaking to fill those gaps?

In facing such central human problems, furthermore, we cannot feign scientific objectivity and disinterest. We may, in fact, well ask in what way we ourselves, perchance, are trying to provide our own substitutes? For does not every claim of having a sanctioned and sure approach to some secrets of nature or existence presuppose a whole new world image with a new kind of priestly practitioner (namely, us) in the centre? Even by offering some insights into the workings of the world views of others, then, we may aim to replace them by the very way we are looking at them. All the more do we have a certain responsibility for being aware of the universal human need for ideological wholeness in general, and, quite particularly, of our own strivings for the restoration or renewal of such wholeness.

It is a persistent part of our task, then, to see where our developmental view may be a source of vital insight in a future world view largely governed by technological and scientific modes of thinking and yet by no means free of the need for a more encompassing orientation. A developmental view must always reassert that while science and technology may give us unheard of powers over the physical universe and over each other, human existence will always begin with the interplay of the newborn's earliest development with society's readiness to 'bring' the new being 'up'. This interplay is subject to such sensitive conditions of strength and weakness that we may well accept human development itself as a kind of revelation concerning our human obligations.

3

The stages of psycho-social development to be discussed here are characterized by crises which must decide the relative fate of developmentally essential human qualities. If I assign to infancy the crisis of 'trust' v. 'mistrust', then, obviously, syntonic trust must prevail; but this can come about only if the infant has also learned, under the guidance of trustworthy parental persons, to develop dystonic mistrust—that is, the rudimentary capacity to discriminate between what is or is not trustworthy and even to be on guard just where one may wish to trust the most. Correspondingly, the lifelong virtue of 'hope' which is to ensue from this earliest stage will come to depend on some experienced capacity not to hope in vain, too much.

As to the kind of parental guidance I have in mind here, however, let me assure you that I do not mean, anywhere in this discourse, an attitude necessarily conscious of the values or, indeed, using the kind of terms discussed here. In any viable culture such guidance is, rather, pervasively offered through an interchange of playful and yet habitual, spontaneous and yet repetitive acts which I call 'ritualizations', following the usage of this term by ethologists in reference to some elaborate patterns of greeting or feeding observed in animals. In humans, ritualizations are repetitive interactions between persons associated with each other in familiar interdependencies, beginning with such simple gestural, facial, and verbal messages as establish or confirm personal bonds and cultural style in everyday activities. However, the way people greet each other or share food, exchange goods, or entertain each other seems entirely 'natural' only to those who share a 'familiar' setting, while its ritualized quality is most obvious to those who are strangers to it and who, in fact, may react to it with some rejectivity, whether they merely experience it as foreign and somewhat overdone or definitely abhorrent in its strangeness. At the same time, ritualized behaviour remains a viable communication (and remains truly 'ritualized') only as long as its formalization yields to some spontaneity on the part of all participants; while it turns into what we would call 'ritualistic' behaviour as soon as the repetitiveness becomes forced, rigid, and one-sided.

What is at stake here can best be demonstrated by an indication of the way in which some seemingly small and playful bits in the earliest ritualized behaviour in life seem to be precursors to lifelong behaviours of great emotional and adaptive significance, all the way to ritual ceremony. As the prone infant looks up and around, he comes to meet in distinct ways, ever again, 'eye to eye' and 'face to face' the inclined countenance of maternal persons. This is, of course, especially pronounced under such conditions as being fed or held. The light in those eyes combines with the music of the voice, which becomes recognizable even as it expresses recognition and attaches names to infant and adult. Now, to have somebody to 'look up to', in general, and, in a variety of settings, to recognize and to be recognized in a ritualized manner remains a basic need of the human being throughout life. It is most expressively reflected, for example, in your very own greeting of *namaste* which combines, with a gesture of bringing the palms together, an intimate meeting of the eyes and a verbal expression of transcendent recognition. Most spontaneously, it reappears universally in the singular way in which lovers 'behold' and address each other, as is expressed in the old song, 'Drink to Me Only With Thine Eyes'. It can be shared by a mass of people who experience a joint fascination in what you call *darshan*, when each individual 'drinks in' the presence of a charismatic leader; and it can be found in the highest expression of faith such as in St Paul's promise that at the moment of death we will come face to face with the divine and that then 'shall we know even as we are known'.

The original nutritional context of such lifelong trust is movingly alluded to in the words of an old Punjabi woman who described the very moment of death to Veena Das: 'It is like being shifted from one breast to the other breast of the mother. The child feels lost in that one instant, but not for long.'

These examples denote the ever-growing dimensions of that basic strength of hope which we assign to the first stage of life and which your scriptures, too, acknowledge as fundamental, for they are central to each individual's sense of 'I' as well as to each communality's sense of 'We', and this, whether the Shining Face and the Hallowed Name reappears in the form of a candle-lit ikon in every dark home, or the sun in the centre of our universe, or as Mao's image on a thousand flags.

The central element of the ritualization of infancy I have called the 'numinous' for reasons which, I hope, have become clear even in my brief list of examples. But each stage and its ritualization is, in turn, related to one of the major human institutions. The numinous remains the special concern of devotional ritual, whether it adheres to institutionalized religion or finds a home in other belief systems.

The power of the loved and admired, the crowned or haloed face as the personification of a shared world image, however, can only be understood if we also realize that the fragmentation or absence of shared ritualization can lead to the most severely disturbed states, as can be seen from the clinical observation that any radical defect in that earliest communication just described can cause—either at the stage itself or in later regressions—the most malignant mental conditions. For each stage of life also harbours, beside a basic syntonic affirmation, a dystonic negation; and in the first stage of life the

3

undue power of such negation is expressed in withdrawal as the most radical form of basic mistrust.

Religious ritual has, for the longest time, counteracted by means of the veneration of founders of unequalled charisma, and by reaffirming the universal power of all syntonic values (we have mentioned only hope, so far), all the dystonic negations which are also reborn with each human being and remain a most destructive part of man's social evolution.

In this connection, it is interesting to note how the world religions utilize, in fact, the earliest and potentially most malignant dystonic trend just described, namely, withdrawal. Self-chosen and joint withdrawal as practised in the many forms of monasticism is ritually combined with the prayerful appeal to the matrix of being, and with a commitment to some form of nurturant service. In the most comprehensive Hindu life plan, in turn, ultimate withdrawal in the normal course of the *ashramas* leads to the *samnyasi's* eventual fusion with *atman*. Thus, each life-time fulfils its own cycle as it joins the cycles of rebirth.

At the same time, we must not forget that religions, as power structures, have often, sooner or later, contributed to the deadliness and murderousness which are apt to accompany the degeneration of meaningful ritualization into excessive and yet confining ritualism; for man's early and lifelong attachment to the numinous has a dystonic counterpart in idolatry and in delusional ways of magic reassurance which are easily misused by false prophets.

4

I have started, as usual, with the first and the most obscure stage of life. If I have succeeded in making it somewhat plausible that the interplay of life cycle and social order begins at the very beginning, we are on our way. I have also indicated that a full report on the stages of life would have to account for all the developmental aspects sketched here for infancy, namely an essential conflict of a syntonic and a dystonic trend (here, basic trust and basic mistrust), a fundamental strength (here, hope) as well as a core-disturbance (withdrawal); a principle of ritualization (here, the numinous) and its interdependence with a major area of social evolution (here, religion). You will thank me, I am sure, for comparing the first and second stage (early childhood) in all these respects only briefly.

To complicate matters, however, not only does each stage bring along its own intrinsic conflict, the transition from one stage to the next can create a developmental crisis by introducing contrasts of overall orientation; as infancy cultivated dependency on creators and providers, early childhood, by contrast, demands a firm measure of independence and self-assertion. In line with cognitive, physiological and psycho-sexual advances, the child is now driven to explore the leeway of the increasingly possible as well as the limits of what is not yet or will never be possible. At the same time, the child comes to experience what is permissible as well as that which is forbidden or exposes one to ridicule, or worse. It will be obvious that the vital possibilities of the second stage depend on the reliability of the gains of the first one.

I have, therefore, called the second psycho-social crisis that of 'autonomy' v. 'shame' and 'doubt' and have claimed for it the rudimentary origin of a healthy 'will', for young children under the impact of the demands of this stage at times alternate between the dangers of becoming too wilful or of being inhibited by a lack of will. The ritualizations, at this stage, are dominated by the discrimination of what can be vigorously affirmed as permissible and possible to persons 'of our kind' and what must be strenuously avoided by them at all costs. The form and the focus of disapproval, of course, differs in different cultures: methods of shaming or of inculcating an early sense of guilt, or of awakening a sense of impurity such as having been polluted or having, in fact, polluted somebody else. The corresponding danger is not only a threat of punishment, however, but also an inner division as well as a demarcation of the world around us into fateful contrasts of good and bad, clean and dirty, beautiful and ugly.

Two reports in our seminar were of special significance in this regard, namely, Veena Das's account of the upbringing of girls among the Punjabis and S. S. Thorat's reminiscences of his childhood in an Untouchable setting permitting the development only of a 'stigmatized identity'. The early emphasis on pollution was illustrated in a scene described by S. S. Thorat, where a small child learning to test the playful properties of a ball must learn the fateful implications of that ball's proximity to the village well; or Veena Das's account of the radically different treatment of a Punjabi girl before and after menstruation. As we study the often abrupt and cruel interferences in each stage, however, it remains for us also to clarify in what way the sequence of all stages may offer, in the long run, compensatory freedoms or associations so that some pervasive meaning—and some measure of free will—may nevertheless seem assured. Some liberations convincingly offered in the distant future—all the way to the next life—may offer some compensations for all the boundaries designating what zones of the body are considered polluted or polluting; what thoughts are thinkable or must be repressed even in phantasy; and what areas of the environment are permissible or out of bounds. For such compensations may not only help to make a much-restricted life liveable, they also may, in rapidly changing times, prove irreplaceable until a truly new world image offers an alternative order. Here, Thorat's report illustrates Ambedkar's genius for energetic re-ritualizing, to the point of adopting another world religion to replace one felt to confirm a fateful stigmatization through hopeless ritualisms. At any rate, in any viable cultural system the rudiments of a sense of free will must emerge with the help of early ritualizations which replace the dystonic trends of wilfulness or lack of will and instead, cultivate some sense of judicious discrimination; and it is this judicious element of ritual which now joins the numinous one. Here we could begin to quote examples of judicious ritualizations and rituals comparable to the ones we have quoted for the numinous trend in life: from the 'Yes' and 'No' pervading daily life in many spheres to the discriminative procedures of the judicial system and to the most exalted judicial aspects (see the 'last judgment') of religious and ideological systems.

To conclude our list, the individual core-pathology arising from an unresolved conflict between wilfulness and over-obedience is that of compulsion and obsession. Correspondingly, the ritualistic trend which emerges where true ritualization weakens appears to be that of legalism, a rule (in small matters or big) by the letter rather than by the spirit, usually abetted by the more obsessive type of person.

Let me now turn even more briefly to the two remaining childhood stages: the play age and the school age. It makes eminent sense that the play age intervenes between the stage when some sense of autonomy and of free will has been established and the school when learning to work becomes a dominant demand. And, indeed, once more we hear the playwright proclaim: 'And one man in his time plays many parts'—thus building a developmental bridge from the free imagination of the play age to the social roles to be experimented with in youth and finally to be 'played' in all seriousness by the adult. At the same time, the child now acquires a miniature world of toys and playgrounds full of people and rules on which *he* can practise ritualizing: for what counts now is the widest imagination permissible and the greatest skill in demonstrating it. This stage adds to man's inner structure a sense not only of the possible but also of the ideal and even the heroic—the Ego-Ideal, in psychoanalytic theory—while it is an essential preparation for an identification with the hierarchy of roles that supports the social structure.

Having written about this a good deal, I will merely add here a word on the school age, where the ritualization of work and of co-operation must synthesize and transcend what has been learned in dealing playfully with objects and ideas—a new task which, contrary to the snail-like reluctance characterizing Shakespeare's schoolboy, has its own fascination. The school age, of course, prepares the child for the basic techniques, the division of labour, and distribution of functions in the prevailing technological system. It is here that ap-prenticeship is rooted: *brahmacharya*, at last.

I may conclude the review of the last two childhood stages by counterpointing to their great developmental potentials their specific ritualizations and ritualisms. The dominant conflict of the play age is 'initiative' v. 'guilt'; its strength, 'purposefulness'. The play age is host to the rudimentary ritualization of the dramatic. The cor-responding terms for the school age are 'industry' v. 'inferiority': 'skill'; and the ritualization of 'formal perfection'. As to the cor-responding pathology, the origins of hysteria were first retraced by Freud to the infantile-genital stage of psycho-sexual development which is also our psycho-social play age; and we can see that a cor-responding ritualism, namely, histrionic dramatism counts on a hysterical trend in adults. Finally, as must be obvious, formalism as a social symptom depends on a compulsive proclivity more or less ready in us all since our school days.

5

To come back to the relationship of life stage and world view, let me (before we reach adolescence and adulthood) counterpoint the tradi-tional Hindu vision with a modern view within which my theory took form. We may well call it American, and yet, it must be entering modern minds and dreams wherever technological and political con-ditions and aspirations impose changes on the ethos of production as well as on that of co-living and education. This, very roughly speak-ing, would be accompanied by a turn in the dominant ethos from

concepts of fate (such as are symbolized in *dharma*) to an individualistic sense of success through progress.

Here, I need only report that when my ideas on the central role of
the stage of identity formation, both in ontogeny and phylogeny,
took hold in my country, I was somewhat shocked by the frequency
with which not only the term identity, but also the other syntonic
psycho-social qualities ascribed by me to various stages, were widely
accepted as conscious developmental 'achievements', while certain
dystonic states (such as identity confusion) were to be totally 'overcome' like symptoms of failure. Thus, my emphasis in each stage on
a built-in and lifelong antithesis ('identity' v. 'identity confusion')
was given a kind of modern Calvinist emphasis. But beyond this,
I gradually realized that the American world view, originally a com-
posite of Biblical and political imageries depicting a promised land
to be reached, in fulfilment of God's will, across some body of water,
had developed into a ready space–time imagery of salvation by
personal and social progress. Each generation of descendants of
immigrants from all the world's nations and creeds had a chance to
become a new and (this is immensely important for the viability of
any new world views) a type of man that could include and absorb
many origins and types; and whose aspirations could be predictably
fulfilled if he only persisted in renewing himself by remaining open to
chances and ready for change.[2]

But even as I write this, I must admit that my first observations
concerning the human life cycle, and especially the syntonic qualities
ascribed to each stage, did have a certain 'optimistic' quality. While
I had, of course, charted them in further pursuit of Freud's first
breakthrough to the infantile stages of psycho-sexual development
and to the early origins of mental disturbances, I had made it my
business to ask: if we know what can go wrong in a given stage, must
it not be possible to define what could have gone right and what, in
fact, are the 'intentions' built by evolution into each given stage, and
into the given sequence of stages? And this *was* in the late forties,
a period when the great 'Midcentury White House Conference' was
in preparation, and its theme was 'A Healthy Personality for Every
Child'. In mentioning all this I am only acknowledging the power of
desha and *kala*, of *shrama* and the *gunas* over any attempt to visualize
and to formulate human life as a whole.

In the study of human development, then, every new concept and
the terms chosen for it will 'naturally' be representative of the world

image within which it originated and of the 'historical moment' when it was formulated. At the same time, it can be shown to have roots in the personal fate of its originator. These interdependencies, however, by no means preclude, in fact they assure, a concept's universal viability. For the problem of identity may vary in intensity or explicitness from one historical moment or from one life history to the next, and yet prove to be essential for human development any time, anywhere, provided that the demonstration of psycho-social and psycho-historical relativity is part of our method. Such inquiry becomes especially important when we are faced with cultural conflicts in our very concepts and terminology: consider the frequent assertion that only westerners as heirs of Judaeo-Christian civilization can experience such guilt as is described clinically in psychoanalytic literature and, for example, ascribed by me as a normative developmental aspect of the stage of initiative. We shall come back to this.

It is not surprising, then, that a seminar like ours in its detailed attempts to isolate and circumscribe acute Indian problems of adulthood with a certain intellectual and scientific precision, always finds itself confronted with the signs and symptoms of a gigantic conflict between age-old and modern determinants of behaviour. In terms of the emphasis or lack of emphasis on particular life stages, questions arose in our seminar such as Dr Ramanujam's clinical inquiry into the question of whether in the India he knows best a circumscribed adolescence marked by conflicts and choices is acknowledged, and the impact such recognition (or, indeed, the lack of it) may have on adulthood. He concludes that in his observation an identity of adjustment rather than of choice is enforced so early that

the social structure does not permit the emergence of a cogent adult role as perceived in western societies. Subordinating one's individual needs to the interests of the group, be it a family, a kinship group, a clan or a class, is upheld as a virtue. . . . Thus, self-assertion becomes selfishness, independent decision making is perceived as disobedience. . . . Under such circumstances it is easier to play safe. The only way this can be accomplished is by passive aggressive behaviour or regression into total passivity.

We are especially grateful for Dr Ramanujam's acknowledgement of the clinical observer's predicament in having to question the values which helped form his own identity. He feels that as a psychiatrist he must point out that

In an agrarian, relatively less competitive social structure where kinship bonds had economic, social, and moral justifications, the values system certainly had a place. In the present day we have to ask if they still fulfil individual and societal needs. The distress caused in individual lives and the fragility of a social structure which can get disorganized at the slightest stress, calls for social scientists to objectively evaluate the present situation.

Or take Veena Das's valuable contribution, which points to the particular complexity of identity formation under the cultural conditions of urban Punjabis where 'it is true that sons are seen as future heirs, and parents look upon them for support in their old age. In contrast, girls are seen as belonging to a different family altogether and their socialization stresses their future roles as wives.' Most remarkable here is the persistence of such cultural patterns under changing modern conditions. But beside these acute problems we may well ask how such a custom as a girl's transfer at the time of her marriage (that is, possibly, at the very beginning of adolescence) to her (previously unknown) husband's family could ever fit into the developmental demands for an identity firm enough to help the girl become a woman ready, in her turn, to become guardian of her sons' as well as her daughters' sense of developmental continuity. Here, the compensations built into the official and the informal structure of the traditional extended family calls for renewed study, and this especially in the light of its waning power.

As we face such cultural and historical relativity, let me assert here only one point which in all the years of work with our scheme has not been weakened: while the exact *age* of onset and the *length* of any stage of development as well as the *intensity* of the conflict experienced may all vary dramatically from one culture to another and from one individual to another, the *order* and *sequence* of these stages remain fixed; for they are intrinsically related both to physiological stages and to the basic requirements of any social order.

By the same token, while I have selected my terms with some care in regard to their translatability, I would welcome any suggestions for more applicable ones in specific contexts, as long as their interrelatedness and the inner order of the whole scheme is safeguarded.

6

From what I have said about the earliest and simplest ritualizations in life, it must be obvious that only adults feeling reasonably at home in the logic of social institutions—and not feeling too unduly discriminated against by the law of the land—can possibly offer, for example, convincing rules of 'Yes' and 'No', of good and bad, of clean and unclean to small children; offer them, that is, with daily ritualizations which, while discouraging excessive wilfulness, do avoid undercutting the developing resources of will-power on which the health of each child and the vitality of the society depends.

In psychoanalysis and in human development we have now, for decades, investigated what the newly-discovered childhood stages may contribute to the strengths and the disturbances in adulthood. But we have only recently come to discuss in earnest, if not without some embarrassment, what an adult really is. It will take many seminars, interdisciplinary and multinational, to clarify this question. Here, it is suggestive to remember the astonishing Marxian prophecy that for human beings to become really adult would mean first to overcome history. It is possible that in the meantime, that is, during the wars of ideological redefinitions of human maturity, youth— periodically, and in some countries—is obliged to carry much, maybe too much, of the burden of ideological change, whether the new generation adjusts (and overadjusts) or revolts (or merely rebels) for a viable identity which is only possible in relative ideological integration, or renewal. For this reason, I have related the crisis of youth (of 'identity' v. 'identity confusion') with the basic human virtue of 'fidelity', which is commitment to a viable world view. This is the place to note, then, that the dystonic counterpart of fidelity is role-refusal, for faith in some roles demands the negation of many others. As to the ritualization governing the adolescent process, I would designate it as ideological, by which I mean a thinking in terms of universal images, whether or not this is part of the effort at thought control within one of the established ideologies. The corresponding adolescent ritualism is represented in the fanatic totalism of oversimplified world views. The core danger of this stage of life arises, for the individual, where inner or outer conditions prevent the formation of a positive identity related to a convincing ideology. The resulting self-negation can evoke near-psychotic conditions.

The resolution of the crisis of youth, obviously, is a preconditon for the two adult stages, the first of which centres in the crisis of 'intimacy' v. 'isolation', and the second in that of 'generativity' v. 'stagnation'. Intimacy is a psycho-social integration of a variety of intimacies, whether in erotic life, in friendship, or, indeed, in work affiliations. The strength to be consolidated in this stage of young adulthood is 'love'. Generativity, in turn, (in all its linguistic and, no doubt, evolutionary ties to genes and generations) must include patterns of procreativity, modes of productivity and various forms of creativity, all fundamental to the central human strength of 'care', the core of householdership. Important among all the forms of generativity, however, is also a continuing self-generation, both in the mature personification of the roles of householdership and (as cultivated in all the world religions and specially also in the Hindu tradition) in the promise of an eventual self-transcendence. But I must name for these stages, too, some dystonic negations: I will call them 'exclusivity' as the counterpart of intimacy, and 'rejectivity' as that of generativity. It is simple enough, and yet can be fateful for individual and society that, as we learn to 'care for', we also learn to exclude; and as we learn to 'take care of' our kind, we are apt to become more rejective of other kinds which we perceive to be a major danger to all that we feel obligated to protect. In fact, this trend adds up significantly to world images in which the grown-ups of our own kind are in a superior category while all others are inferior, that is, lower. To this overall human trend I have applied the term 'pseudo-speciation', for we are inclined to view our own kind as *the* select and elect human species, and all others, as more or less undesirable ones. Unnecessary to say, in this rejection of otherness humans can become ferocious, and systematically so. Now that we have invented the most systematic means of total destruction on the largest scale, nothing is more dangerous to the human species as a whole than this irrational tendency of pseudo-speciation. It is all the more important to understand the psychological implications of the way in which ancient systems have attempted to find solutions for man's traditional divisiveness. Your caste system, again, deserves study, as it institutionalizes this trend by giving it a pervasive logic crowned by a cosmic process which promises to the lowest, too, equality—if only in the very long run; even as the Christian world image promises an eventual and universal Caritas to make up for the lack of care received by the poor of this earth: 'and the last shall be first'.

In one of my books I have attempted, as far as a westerner and a psychoanalyst can undertake such a task, to explain to my students and readers in what way Gandhi's Truth Force is the most important step towards a joint political and religious transcendence of such exclusivity and rejectivity, and a step which is a model of integration of an 'old-time religion' with modern politics. However, such a force must always wait for its leader and for its historical moment and even then it cannot, as history has shown so blatantly, exclude the temporary regression to reciprocal mass-annihilations. What we can learn from this is that a markedly moralistic suppression of man's dystonic qualities cannot overcome them in the long run: they can only be contained and transcended by an ethical affirmation which tunes the traditional to modern insight and thus is more than a negation of a negation.

But let me conclude by airing a more recent impression. One of the most fateful issues before the world is that of the control of the number of births, that is, a wise allocation of generative needs: a problem obviously calling for an ethical position within a new world image wide and strong enough to absorb age-old beliefs and prejudices. May I, as a visiting American, mention the fact that in the impressive and colourful procession of floats in your recent Republic Day Parade (it was my third one) there was one that depicted as an ideal a 'smaller and happier family' consisting of a pair of parents and one boy, one girl. As one to whom the 'pursuit of happiness', together with life and liberty (and, so some add, property), is constitutionally guaranteed, I found this pictorial theme and that phraseology almost too familiar. But what, I could not help asking, could it mean to the masses of India in their present predicament between two technological eras? And if we do believe in the control of births, must not this principle be formulated, for all of us, in terms more universal than 'each family for itself'? Here we may apply the concept of generativity to the political question as to whether an issue of such ancient depth can be solved by an approach merely imposing statistical limits on an aspect of life fortified by a combination of deep-seated natural and religious needs. Must not the quantitative issue be formulated qualitatively, and re-ritualized with insight and persuasion, from the village up, and out? This float, to be sure, attempted to do so by advocating happiness, but, so it seems, for the few. If fewer births are a goal to be reached with the need for generativity intact and without a new, a statistical, kind of rejectivity, this can only mean a commitment to better chances to develop the human potential of all the children born, anywhere within one's political orbit. That such care, reaching into the earliest stages, is one of the conditions of holding together the social fabric and working toward a species-wide world view of the future, that I have attempted to make plausible today on theoretical grounds.

7

I now have sketched prospectively some of the indispensable meanings which the earliest experiences of the smallest child must have for the most comprehensive world views; I have reviewed the relativity of the adolescent position; and I have submitted a few new ideas about the stage of life which is hardest to grasp for the adult, namely, adulthood. Let me, in conclusion, refer to the retrospection in late life on lives nearly concluded; and since I have found it difficult to expose you to so many systematic pronouncements without being able to refer to examples from life histories, let me, in conclusion, tell you about an experience we had in our seminar with two great moving pictures: Ingmar Bergman's *Wild Strawberries* and Pattabhi Rama Reddy's *Samskara*.

While Bergman wrote his own screen-play, *Samskara* is, of course, the filmed version of Anantha Murthy's book, written in Kannada. Murthy, in our seminar, shared with us some profound thoughts on language and identity from the point of view of an Indian author who persists in writing in his own regional language, accessible as it is only to a small populace with very limited literacy. It was, therefore, especially interesting to view the themes of his novel as depicted in the universal imagery of an Indian motion picture and to compare them with corresponding themes in the European movie. Here, my own conclusions must be considered most tentative.

Now, I know that it is very difficult to imagine a moving picture one has not seen, but I will try to proceed under the assumption that most of you have either seen one of the two pictures, or will do so soon. In either case, you will know that the 'language' of a moving picture includes (to quote from a letter of Satish Bahadur, who attended some of our meetings) 'cinematic construction, plot relationships, cinematic transitions, values of camera composition, lighting, locations, properties in the camera frame and the value of the spoken words'. Using such a medium, it is the film director's artfulness that permits him to present to us in a few hours 'a variety of persons of different ages in acute life crises in a sequence of short scenes which typify the whole course of their lives so vividly that we viewers are sure we have "met" them, both on the screen and in ourselves'.[3]

Dr Borg, the Swedish doctor, and Praneshacharya, the South Indian Brahmin, are not the same age: the first is most definitely old, the second, for reasons of his own, prematurely ageing. They both face a corresponding crisis, however. Both are highly honoured professional men. Dr Borg, in fact, is about to receive Sweden's highest medical award, an honorary doctorate in the Cathedral of Lund, while Praneshacharya finds himself increasingly recognized as an outstanding member of a Brahmin élite. But, alas, both of them are faced, in the true sense of the word, with the image of a dead man, in whom they recognize themselves. Dr Borg, in an elaborate dream, sees below him a shattered coffin out of which his own corpse reaches toward him 'smiling scornfully'. Awakened, the doctor feels that, 'It is as if I'm trying to say something to myself which I don't want to hear when I'm awake.'[4]

Praneshacharya, however, is confronted with another man's corpse: Naranappa is one of the first victims of the plague which is about to take over their territory. He had been shunned by the Brahmin community because of his deviationist habits, including an affair with a low-caste girl, Chandri. The community is debating passionately whether or not he now deserves to be cremated as a Brahmin: and Praneshacharya, the exalted, is to make the decision. This, incidentally, gives this film its name, 'Samskara', which, so we decided in our seminar, means 'the right rite at the right time'. But Praneshacharya suddenly recognizes himself in the dead man as he realizes that he, himself, would have liked to do, if he had only dared, some of what the dead man had done. So he, too, must admit to himself that he has not lived, is not ready for the conclusion of life. It would be mere ritualism, then, on Praneshacharya's part, to deny a full ritual cremation to Naranappa for doing what Praneshacharya feels was part of his own unlived life. Strangely enough, this formulation makes sense in Dr Borg's life, too; for if in some vital respects he has not lived, is not the elaborate professional coronation about to take place a ritualism with little meaning?

I would not hesitate to see in the conflicts of both men an old age crisis (in Praneshacharya's case, to be sure, somewhat premature) of 'integrity' v. 'despair'. It is their special sense of integrity which prevents both men from accepting unthinkingly the role of the great doctor or the righteous Brahmin and which forces them to face their inner despair. For in our terms, only facing old age despair with integrity will permit a person to fulfil, at the end of life, his share of universal wisdom, and to outlive the last dystonic affects: disgust and disdain, including self-disdain. Old age despair, in turn, is always involved with that part of the past in which the person has 'lived off' a role chosen or foisted on him while leaving some essential aspects of himself unlived. In our two heroes it is by no means accidental that the unlived portion of their lives appears to be related to generativity: in their roles as medical and priestly caretakers of others they have left the more intimate matters of caring unfulfilled.

In Dr Borg's case this becomes clear when we hear that he, who has survived innumerable siblings, has only one son, who is so far childless. Now the son's wife who is visiting the old doctor is pregnant for the first time. His son, a doctor like himself, but more knowingly desperate, wishes her to abort the foetus, for he does not wish to commit himself to procreation, and this clearly as a consequence of his father's neglect of emotional matters in the pursuit of his career. The young woman, however, wants to give birth to the child and hopes to gain Dr Borg's support by facing him with his and his son's problems, which, more obviously in the son than in the father, include some self-rejection: for an arrest in generativity always also leads to a neglect of further self-generation. Praneshacharya's marriage, too, is childless for as a youth of eighteen he married a crippled girl of twelve. He has taken care of her most diligently, even as he has been a most conscientious Brahmin scholar and priest; but he has neglected the mutuality of intimacy as well as the sensual balance of life. Now, the young woman outcaste who was Naranappa's mistress not only wishes to have a relationship with Praneshacharya but also wants desperately to bear him a child. In both cases, then, the unlived life is the commitment to procreation.

What I could hope to offer here is only a brief comparison of the two men's dominant life problems. I cannot here follow through, as it would well deserve, another theme which is basic to both pictures. Both men engage in a journey, a kind of pilgrimage back into their lives, and beyond them. Dr Borg, on a slow car trip to Lund, stops at the summer home of his childhood and visits the strawberry patch which gives the movie its name: for there, in his youth, he had seen his passionate childhood love ·being seduced by his brother, an experience which had confirmed, as it were, the isolation of his childhood and had later made him essentially exclusive and rejective in spite of a notable career. He has a number of chance encounters, drops in to visit his mother, now cold and isolated, and acquires some young travel companions noisily caught in the crises of youth. As I have outlined in a lengthy paper,[5] each of the persons (or groups of persons) encountered on the journey and in his dreams faces him with the joys and the sorrows of one of the stages of life and especially with its unlived portions. Finally arriving in Lund, he passes through the great ceremony as through a dream: the day's insights concerning his life are now more real than its crowning event. All this makes this moving picture a most enlightening medium of instruction in the problems of the life cycle in the West.

As to *Samskara*, Praneshacharya, on his journey, encounters primarily two youthful persons: he meets Chandri in the woods, where they consummate their sexual union, and he too acquires a young travelling companion, a strangely concrete, even humorous young man, with his identity defined by the possibilities of social reality. He represents, so it seems, Praneshacharya's alter ego, an alternate identity sacrificed in his youth for the course of life for which he now receives acclaim. At a crossing, these two suddenly separate, and Praneshacharya continues his pilgrimage, markedly alone and, so it seems, open to some late choices which may present themselves as genuine.

Only an intensive discussion would permit us to come to a convincing comparison of differences and similarities in the fates of the two men. Both, of course, belong, and most consciously so, to the studious élite and the trusted caretakers among their people (élites, no doubt, given to some special scruples), thus arousing our, and probably the filmmaker's, intense identification. Thus, if our logic of the life cycle is pervasive and convincing in both of these works, this may, to some extent, be due to the way we educated people think, and especially speak, of life. But the artfulness of both works surpasses such critical issues and would permit us, if time permitted, to enlarge on wider cultural and even universal comparisons. For even as the two life cycles are outlined convincingly, so also can we recognize the two world views which form their matrix. The Lutheran version insists that (as an examiner tells Dr Borg in one of his dreams) 'a doctor's first duty is to ask forgiveness', meaning, of course, for his neglect of his beloved ones; while the Hindu version asserts that a man's neglect of as fundamental an aspect of life as sensuality (*kama*) leaves him incomplete in the fulfilment of his *dharma*. Dr Borg, in conclusion, is shown as a man who, having found and relived his conflicts, has sensed forgiveness and regained some of the peace and innocence of his childhood. His life cycle, indeed, has come to a close; while in a series of very concrete small acts and words exchanged with his reunited son and daughter-in-law he mends, as it were, the generational cycle: hope, indeed, for the child to be born. As Praneshacharya walks out of his picture, one feels that a number of as yet undefined new cycles—of restitution and of transcendence—have been reopened.

The comparison of two such pictures, then, permits the demonstration of the complementarity of new and old world views dominating contemporary life cycles. For this we thank the writers and directors who, we conclude, by giving convincing form to unformulated conflicts, help to re-ritualize human endeavours which have been rigidified by ritualism.

All this, I wish we could discuss with Vikram Sarabhai. For he, as few others, could show us the interrelation of our thinking with the demands of a new universal world view: science and technology. We deeply miss him, even as we feel his pervading presence in our deliberations.

NOTES AND REFERENCES

1. Quoted in Gerald Holton, *Thematic Origins of Scientific Thought*, Cambridge, Mass., Harvard University Press, 1973, p. 359.
2. I may say in passing how much one can learn in an election year about the ingrown overall pattern of a country's hopes and fears which reaches from the deeply pre-rational and irrational into the most conscious political manipulation. At any rate, in my country one president after another has proclaimed what has most fittingly been called a secular-religious faith, prophesizing a new era such as the 'New Deal' or the 'New Frontier.' We expect at this very moment the announcement of a 'New Spirit'.
3. Erik H. Erikson, 'Reflections on Dr. Borg's Life Cycle', *Daedalus*, Spring 1976, p. 3.
4. Ibid., p. 1.
5. Ibid.

II. Identity and Adulthood

3

TOWARD MATURITY

Problems of Identity seen in the Indian Clinical Setting

B. K. RAMANUJAM

In 'Reflections on Dr Borg's Life Cycle', Erikson comments: 'But then we must consider how long it took enlightened humanistic and scientific mankind to acknowledge and chart the existence of developmental stages—physical and emotional, cognitive and social—in childhood and youth, not to speak of the highly diverse history of the treatment of children through the ages, a creature existing and developing at the whim of fate—and of the adults. No doubt there has been a deep-seated adult resistance (first discovered and explained by Freud) not only to the remembrance of one's own childhood, but also to the recognition in children of developmental potentials which may upset the adult conviction of occupying in the universe a safe and sanctioned place with a well defined point of view.'[1] Implicit in this statement is the idea that at last this resistance has been overcome and there is an acknowledgement of the existence of the developmental stages of childhood and youth. In Indian society it is doubtful if such a clear-cut acknowledgement exists. As far as our clinical experience suggests, only childhood is recognized as a developmental phase. I suspect that this may be an urban, middle class value orientation, though I understand from one of my sociologist colleagues that the childhood phase is also recognized in the rural areas. Adolescence as a distinct phase, however, is not identified. Since my experience in clinical work is limited to an urban population, my comments should be viewed within this frame of reference.

According to Erikson, 'Identity, to be sure, does not originate (and does not end) in adolescence: from birth onward, the child learns what counts in his culture's space–time and life plan, by the

community's differential responses to his maturing behaviour. He
learns to identify with ideal prototypes and to develop away from
evil ones. But identity formation comes to a decisive crisis in youth—
a crisis *alleviated* or *aggravated* by different societies in different
ways.'[2] I would emphasize the phrases 'alleviated' or 'aggravated' as
of significance in our context. If there is recognition of adolescence
as a distinct developmental phase, society will afford opportunities
to the young to work through this phase to attain adult identity. In
the absence of such recognition an individual has to struggle alone.
Finding his own coping devices and depending upon how successful
these are, he will feel competent or incompetent in his adult role. In
the traditional Indian social matrix, even though adolescence as a
phase was not recognized, the passage from childhood to the adult
stage was guided through a series of what Erikson would call 'situations', the ultimate goal being the establishment of an individual in
his adult role. In the current context, I feel that our whole socio-
cultural milieu is in transition. The accepted value systems and
identification patterns are in a flux which results in considerable
confusion and in some cases results in psychopathological manifestations. In this paper I propose to discuss how identity conflicts come
to the fore during the psychotherapeutic process.

Case Notes

1. N., a 24-year-old single young man with post-graduate qualifica-
tions in chemical engineering, diagnosed as a borderline patient, was
referred to us because of his repeated failure to keep a job. Most of
these jobs were secured through his father's influence. The father,
not so unconsciously, had communicated to the patient that he was
endowed with superior abilities and merited a responsible senior
position in industry. This was what the father expected of his son
because he himself was a successful businessman in spite of a limited
education. The patient readily fell into this role and whenever he was
employed, he acted during the first few days as if he was competent
to make policy decisions which resulted in his services being ter-
minated. When this patient was first admitted to our day hospital,
he refused to identify himself as a patient and went about telling
others that he was my colleague and was helping me in my work.
After about two months he became very depressed and apathetic. In
the treatment sessions, he confided that he was concerned about his

father's ambitions and subsequent disappointment at his failure. Since he was, more or less, considered incompetent he decided to prove that he was so. He said, 'Doctor, you treat my father. He gets very worried about me. He says I am useless and he is right.' If we ignore the diagnostic label we can perceive a process which had its origin long before the patient came for clinical attention. The concern in this case was not for his own role responsibility but for his father's anxiety. It was almost as if his very existence did not matter except for the sake of his father's well-being. This is a big load to carry for any individual. We come across this phenomenon repeatedly where an overwhelming guilt aborts all attempts at finding one's own individual role in the family matrix. As Erikson has pointed out, 'A state of acute identity diffusion usually becomes manifest at a time when the young individual finds himself exposed to a combination of experiences which demand his simultaneous commitment to physical intimacy (not by any means always overtly sexual), to decisive occupational choice, to energetic competition, and to psychosocial self-definition.'[3]

2. A more dramatic instance is of a 43-year-old man, married and with two children, who was forced by his wife to live separated from the joint family after several years of living together because of her low status in the household. He, very reluctantly, agreed to separate but maintained his links by deciding to have dinner with his parents every day. He would insist on visiting his parents with his wife, on his way to a social function, a movie or an evening at the club, and report to them on his return that he was going home. This may illustrate the point I am making in an exaggerated form, but variations on this theme are seen in many cases where, ostensibly, the establishment of a separate household has been accepted but the emotional ties remain as strong as ever. As Ben Schlesinger has observed, 'It seems that physically the nuclear family, composed of parents and their unmarried children, is slowly coming into being; but in most cases the obligations and relationships of the joint family are emotionally and morally retained in varying degrees. This is almost a social and economic necessity, in the absence of adequate substitutes for the old family functions. And this in the long run may pave the way for a new pattern for the nuclear family, different from the more or less individualistic ideal of the West.'[4]

David B. Lynn states, 'First, for the wife, the husband may provide love, emotional support, and companionship. There is evidence that where the husband is absent women may focus too narrowly on their children, to the detriment of their development. The evidence suggests that, when the husband is absent, the mother may both burden her child with adult problems and at the same time over-protect him and encourage his dependence on her.... There is evidence suggesting that, where the father is absent the boy (a) is more immature; (b) shows poor age–mate adjustment; (c) is insecure in his identification with his father, and so strives more strongly towards masculine identification; (d) lacks a masculine model in the home (the father) and hence his masculine behaviour is largely bravado.'[5] Lynn's studies are from broken homes and conducted in a different socio-cultural context. Interestingly, with minor modifications his conclusions can apply to many situations we see in our clinical work where the father is away from home most of the time. In these cases, the fathers are very involved in their vocations and have little time to spare for the family. Children from such families are brought to the clinic for either poor scholastic performance or behaviour problems of varying severity. When we first see them they are very passive, inhibited and reluctant to involve themselves in goal-directed tasks. Only after considerable time they form a relation-ship with the therapist. One significant feature repeatedly noted is their great reluctance to express any negative feelings towards their fathers. In some cases these feelings are transferred on to teachers, but in most cases the aggression shows itself in play. We have been impressed by the phenomenon that the commonest play item chosen by boys in our play room is the toy gun. This is despite the fact that our children are not so exposed to the theme of cowboys or Red Indians.

In such cases we learn from the anamnesis that the father is a distant figure. He is not an object with whom the child can be close, but who periodically appears on the scene and remains aloof or reprimands the child for various acts of commission and omission. It has been brought to my attention by professional colleagues brought up in villages that this is the paradigm of the relationship between father and son in rural areas.[6] Since the mother feels equally neglected, she colludes with the child's negative feelings towards the father to form a dyadic relationship.

3. Mr B., a 36-year-old, educated, sophisticated salesman in a commercial firm, came for help because whenever he was forced to be in the same room with authority figures he could not help but pass flatus. This, necessarily, prevented him from attending meetings and conferences with his superiors. In spite of being a very talented and competent person he could never aspire for responsible positions which he deserved and desired. He had resigned himself to remaining in a junior position for years whereas his juniors had moved on. During treatment his dread of his father when he was young came to light. His father image was that of a stern, authoritarian individual whose only interaction with the patient was during meal times when a very rigid code of table manners was enforced. The mother went along with these disciplinary measures and reinforced the dread of the father. I may add that she herself was in awe of her husband. As he became an adult, the patient organized his life style in such a way that it demanded limited interpersonal interaction. After his routine work he would come home and lie on his bed reading mystery novels until it was time to have his dinner and go to bed. His wife had to adjust to this mode of life. He had decided not to have any children. Thus we see that he had adopted a routine which can be termed 'regressed', demanding little of him as a husband and head of a household. As Erikson has stated, 'From a genetic point of view, then, the process of identity formation emerges as an evolving configuration—a configuration which is gradually established by successive ego syntheses and resyntheses throughout childhood. It is a configuration gradually integrating constitutional givens, idiosyncratic libidinal needs, favoured capacities, significant identifications, effective defenses, successful sublimations, and consistent roles.'[7] In the example given above we can see that there was minimal opportunity for ego-synthesis due to non-gratification of affectional needs, and significant identifications. The defence system was ineffective and the patient had compromised in fulfilling his adult role by restricting his role functions to the minimum.

4. A rather different picture is presented by a 26-year-old married businessman who came for help because he had woven around himself so many restrictions based upon superstitions that his business was affected. He would study the planetary constellation for the day and determine the number of auspicious hours when he could conduct his business transactions. If he had an appointment at a pre-

determined time, he would either postpone it or cancel it if he heard someone sneezing even at a distance. A cat crossing the road was, of course, a bad omen. One can see how he had restricted his whole life-style to suit the whims of supernatural forces. There was a reason for his feeling of absolute vulnerability. He was the only son born to a consumptive father who, for reasons of health, had to stay away from home ever since the patient's childhood. He was under the care of servants and relatives. He was permitted to see his father only once a week for fear of contagion. His guardians, who pitied his plight, pampered him, so much so that he was literally spoon-fed until he was twelve or thirteen years old. The rest of the time he was left to his own devices. When he was fifteen years old his father died. His paternal uncle who became his guardian, lived for a few years and died leaving a son and a daughter. The patient found himself the head of a household and also a businessman in his own right without any experience at the age of twenty. A family myth became established that all male members of the family die young leaving a single male issue to perpetuate the family tree. This patient had no parental figures in his formative years to form significant identification patterns. He felt he was a victim of forces beyond his control. The only way he could cope with this predicament was by developing faith in supernatural forces and propitiating them all the time. In his day-to-day life he depended upon other people's good will and generosity for survival. To this end, he went out of his way to be gracious. People took advantage of his vulnerability which lowered his self-esteem. He became very dissatisfied with himself, with his difficulty in asserting himself and a lack of meaningful life goals. Being an intelligent person despite a limited education, he came for help on his own.

Here one can see a situation where the very people in the environment who offer a continuity of existence are absent. With whom does one identify? How do the conflicts get resolved? How does one perceive one's identity where all the parameters are vague and diffuse? In the traditional joint family system substitute objects were available who could compensate, however inadequately, and provide significant objects for identification. I would prefer to use 'transitional' instead of 'substitute', because objects other than parents, no matter how effective they are, are not totally acceptable. They can never really fulfil the affectional needs. I present the following case material in support of this hypothesis.

5. A child of nine was brought for evaluation because of aggressive behaviour and poor performance in school. On evaluation he was found to be above average in intelligence. However, his involvement in performing given tasks was minimal and he showed lack of interest. He was very guarded about giving any clue to his feelings concerning other members of the family. In his case history, it was found that he was taken by his grandparents to live with them when he was a few months old, as he was their first grandson and his mother was considered too young to look after him. His mother and a younger sibling visited him once a year during holidays. The grandparents reported that whenever he was asked if he would like to go back to his parents he would deny such a wish. They provided a good and loving environment at home. According to the grandparents everything a child could wish for was provided. But his silent resentment was manifested in his unwillingness to fulfil their expectations. A passive aggressive behaviour was the only outlet available to him. We have seen several such children who are extremely reluctant to admit that they miss their parents. It takes a long time for them to admit that they resent the fact that their parents have abandoned them while their siblings live with the parents. I have dwelt on this topic at length as this phenomenon is not uncommon. Either for financial reasons, or in the interest of educating them, or as a generous gesture towards a barren relative, children are often sent away by their parents. Obviously, they have no say in the matter and their feelings do not count. We have instances where, in an extended family, even in the presence of parents an aunt or an uncle assumes the *de facto* parental role. At the time of evaluation the aunt or the uncle provides the developmental history while the mother sits passively. Whenever we have attempted to modify this pattern by bringing the parents to recognize their appropriate role the treatment is discontinued. I was very curious to see if this conflict-ridden situation leaves residues in adult life. The fact that such children grow into adults carrying problems of identity was brought home to me by two adult patients.

6. A. came to my attention when he was 19 years old. The problem which brought him to the clinic was that he could not concentrate on his studies. The reason for his difficulty was his fear that the Goddess Amba (referring to a photograph) was always watching him. Any 'evil thought' which crossed his mind would be immediately

detected and she would punish him. He attempted to cope with this fear by turning his back to the framed photograph of Amba in his room. This did not bring relief and he had to turn the photograph towards the wall. Finally, he had to remove the picture and put it away because an anger towards Amba was mounting within him. This young man came from a family of nine that included his parents and six siblings. He was taken away by his paternal grandparents at the age of eight months as they were lonely. The parents and siblings lived in the same town and he would visit them on weekends and holidays. He was perceived by the family as an obedient and conformist child. His self-perception was that of a dutiful,. conscientious individual. His problems started at adolescence. His grandparents were conservative, puritancial people. However, they made considerable sacrifices to provide him with the reasonable comforts a lower middle-class family can afford, and a good education. He was very grateful to them for what they had done for him. Soon after evaluation he was taken up for treatment by one of our staff members. He attended a few sessions and then dropped out. He came back again when he was twenty-four. By then he had completed his Master's degree and secured a job. What surprised me was the fact that soon after he completed his education and was employed, he decided to leave his grandparents and go back to his parents. At the time of re-evaluation he told me that all these years he had never reconciled himself to his separation from his parents. As long as he was a dependent individual there was nothing he could do about his choice of residence. As soon as he was employed and became independent he exercised his privilege and went back to his parents. He provided monetary support to his transitional parents and also supported his own parents. This prevented them from raising any objections. He, however, was dissatisfied with himself. For the sake of appearances he was fulfilling his adult role obligations. He, however, was very unsure of himself and before committing himself to marriage and family wanted to be sure of his own identity. (The choice of the term 'identity' is mine, to indicate the sum and substance of his conflict.)

7. The same conflict can be seen in another situation, which clinically manifested itself differently. An educated married woman of thirty sought consultation because of marital conflict due to sexual incompatibility. At the time of referral she was the mother of a six-

year-old boy. She was the eldest of three children, the only girl, and was taken away by an unmarried aunt in infancy. She was brought up by this aunt and a bachelor uncle who shared the house. According to her she had all the love and affection one could wish for. However, there were very strict taboos in this household about sexual matters. She was not permitted to play with boys. At the age of eleven when she started menstruating she was made to feel that this was an unavoidable misfortune which she had to endure. From then on she was prohibited even to touch a boy during play as this would be considered most improper and allegedly result in dire consequences. At the age of sixteen she was brought back by her parents in preparation for marriage. Her parents were total strangers to her as until then she had visited them only occasionally during holidays. Thus, during adolescence she came to live in a strange house among strangers. The father was a distant figure. The mother, an epileptic, exploited the situation by holding out threats that the father would be angry for her various misdeeds. She lived in constant dread of doing something wrong until she was married off at the age of nineteen against her wishes. Without any meaningful communication with her parents or a healthy peer group relationship, she found escape in a rich fantasy life. Marriage to her meant rescue by a man who would love her, shower her with warmth and affection, be understanding and make no demands. The sexual demands made by her husband after marriage came as an emotionally traumatic experience. She would yield after great resistance but the coital experience would leave her frustrated and embittered. Pregnancy came as a shock and the whole period including delivery was an agonizing experience. After the birth of the child she vowed never to become pregnant again. Although she felt affection for the child, she could not caress him or tolerate any bodily contact with him. By the time she came for help, her marital relationship had deteriorated considerably. She verbalized her predicament as, 'My husband does not love me. He only loves my body and therefore I cannot forgive him.' This same person could go into ecstasies when imagining a whole sequence of romantic interludes with a man leading to a climactic experience without actual coitus.

We can see here an example where the environment had a profound effect on the patient's role percept. The only substitute parental figures with whom she could identify because they fulfilled her need for affection, were unmarried, and they constantly undermined sexuality as vulgar and degrading and extolled the platonic concept of love and affection without physical contact. As she grew up, her biological-emotional needs were like those of any other woman. Being an attractive person she attracted the attention of many men, but when they responded she would react with disgust and anger. She could accept a relationship only at an intellectual level. For all practical purposes she fulfilled the role of a wife, a mother and a competent housewife; but the inner uncertainties plagued her constantly, so that neither could she give without reserve nor find gratification in receiving. Her whole concept of herself and the world around her was overly romanticized and face to face with reality she suffered profound feelings of inadequacy which she rationalized by perceiving the environment as selfish and nongiving. Once, during the therapy sessions, she asked 'Why do I have such an insatiable craving for love and affection?' Obviously, in my presentation here, the whole therapeutic process which brings the conflict of identity to the fore cannot be reproduced. My attempt has been to emphasize that such conflicts are frequently seen in individuals, children, adolescents and adults. It may be argued that people seen in a clinical set up are necessarily conflict-ridden and this need not represent what is happening in a socio-cultural milieu. In the following observations I propose to argue that such disturbances are not limited to a few individuals but reflect the existing socio-cultural flux in Indian society.

Erikson says, 'There are, however, periods in history which are relative identity vacuums and in which three forms of human apprehension aggravate each other: fears aroused by discoveries and inventions (including weapons) which radically expand and change the whole world image, anxieties aggravated by the decay of institutions which have been the historical anchor of an existing ideology, and the dread of an existential vacuum devoid of spiritual meaning.'[8] I submit that at present we are witnessing such an 'identity vacuum' in Indian history. This is manifested in manifold ways. Over the years we have seen in our clinical work a manifestation of depression which I feel is a phenomenon of 'anomie'. Typically these are of young people who come to us with complaints of inability to concentrate, a general feeling of loneliness with concomitant symptoms of loss of appetite, sleeplessness, etc. A typical young man of this *genre* comes from a village. He is a first generation student. His parents are illiterate farmers or artisans. His siblings may have gone through the exercise of going to school but have left school by the third or fourth grade and gone into the family occupation. Our client is an exception. He does well in school. After completing primary education he goes to the nearest town for secondary education. He is intelligent, and performs very well academically. He completes his high school creditably. All the family resources are pooled together to send him to college in the city. He has been brought up to believe that he is something special. His parents, his siblings and others in his home town go to great lengths in financing his education. He comes to the college in the city. His alienation from his roots has three distinct phases. When he first comes to the city he is full of self-confidence. Very soon he is very homesick. He visits his home at every available opportunity and looks forward to his vacations. By the time he has finished his second term he is not so enthusiastic about his visits home, and they are shortened. After a year he finds excuses not to go home. He feels very guilty but has enough rationalizations. But these are not convincing and the conflict emerges. From a situation where he was the star of the show he comes to an environment where he has to compete with many equals and even superiors to hold his own. Added to this is the fact that in comparison to his city peers he is seen as a country bumpkin. The sudden deflation of self-image is devastating. Initially he goes home to find comfort, security and a sense of belonging. But he is a stranger in his own environment. He is the educated, city-bred, sophisticated, all-knowing person. His uneducated parents cannot claim to advise him. They look up to him for enlightenment. There is a subtle message that he is superior and that they have invested all they have so that he succeeds. This is a burden which is a deadweight. He cannot tell them that he is lonely and comes back so that he can derive strength from them. But, alas, their image of him is that of a strong self-dependent person. He goes back to the city utterly helpless. He wants to justify their trust and confidence in him. He is angry that they have placed such a burden on him. He cannot afford to be angry because they have given him everything. These young people are defeated, helpless, lonely, looking for someone who will understand this dilemma, uncritically and without condescension. They are not ready to make decisions. Their elders, the decision makers, feel that they are incompetent to make decisions for their 'educated son'. Thus they find themselves totally estranged from their own environment and they do not have a place in the environment which has fallen to their lot. This situation symbolizes a crisis occurring on a much larger scale and needs to be considered in a developing society like India where more and more people are migrating to the cities for education, where they find themselves isolated.

In Indian society the daughter-in-law–mother-in-law conflicts are well known. The fact which needs to be emphasized is that the traditional concept of mutual adaptation, at least tolerance, is not operating as well as it once did. Whenever this is expected, the price paid for maintaining a semblance of harmony is very high. It is generally believed that Indian women are passive. I would like to offer a different perspective on this so-called passivity. It has been repeated often enough that the woman is dependent on a male in all stages of life—a father in childhood, a husband during adulthood and a son during old age. This calls for remarkable adaptational capacities in any human being. If one's continued role status depends upon the whims of others, one has to guard it by all possible means. I feel the woman accomplishes this by very subtle manipulations. She is the passive one but she also determines the level of intimacy, gratification of affectional needs and assurance of relative harmony in the family. In this dynamic process the son has a pivotal role. The daughter has to marry and leave home anyway. Thus she cannot be counted upon to play a significant role, whereas it is the son who maintains the continuity of the mother's existence. She cannot alienate his sympathies. Dominance–submission is one coordinate of this interaction pattern. If this does not work, a more subtle and more sure method is the generation of shame–guilt component. Working with male children we see that their sense of loyalty is so great that they reject any probing or interpretation of their anger towards their mothers. Sometimes it is relatively more readily accepted towards fathers. Behaviourally, aggression may be directed towards the mother but at a conscious level this is not acceptable. This is seen in a different context from the mother's point of view. She can tolerate aggressive behaviour but is shocked if a child verbally expresses hostility and wishes of death. The feeling towards the father is an ambiguous one. He is either idealized or perceived as an object of contempt for his passivity. He is seen to be a straw hero who struts about dominating vulnerable, defenceless children. This does not mean that he is not feared and obeyed, but the motivating factor is not respect for his authority. If these are the models for identification, one can well imagine what kind of integrated personalities will develop!

The consequences of this parental constellation are seen in adolescents perhaps a little less obviously than in adults. I have already pointed out that adolescence as a distinct developmental phase is an artifact in India. This is purely an urban phenomenon influenced by mass media. Traditionally, one does not hear about an adolescent culture. In the village society, after one has emerged from childhood, one passes through adolescence learning the skills of adult responsibilities. It is not a privileged position in our socio-cultural setting. Even in the urban lower-middle and middle classes, the constant emphasis is to learn and become competent to share the burden of family maintenance as soon as possible. I must admit, however, that the psychological problems which, from western orientation, should be resolved by an individual during adolescence, spill over into his adult life. For quite some time we at the B. M. Institute have been toying with the concept of extended adolescence. This occurred to us because many of the acting out behaviours we see even in late adulthood are characteristic of an adolescent pattern. If we accept the thesis that conflicts appropriate to a particular phase of development should be resolved, at least to some extent, before moving on to the next stage, it is understandable that since a culture does not recognize adolescence as a distinct phase, no provision is made to facilitate the resolution of such conflicts. It is only natural that these conflicts should be seen in adulthood.

We have to view the process of identity formation in a much larger cultural context. In a society where assertion of individuality is not a cherished value, but conformity to a group value system in order to maintain group identity is the ideal, the process of identity formation, perhaps, is different. For example, the understanding of the whole process of mothering in early childhood is based on the assumption of prolonged breast feeding which, by itself, does not mean much. Even prolonged breast feeding as a common phenomenon is not borne out by our studies. We have found eight months to be the average. Weaning is abrupt and the measures used are anything but conducive to a smooth transition. Application of bitter tasting preparations to the nipples, separation from the mother temporarily, are the most frequent measures adopted. When we explore the child's reactions to such weaning methods, invariably the response is that the child does not show any reaction. Is it that the Indian child's coping devices are particularly effective, or that the mothers are insensitive to the child's needs? Is this a situation which is conducive to the development of 'basic trust'?

We have, unfortunately, very little information about the anal muscular maturation stage. The oft-quoted statements of permissiveness regarding bowel and bladder training give us no clues. In our middle class sample we got very little information in this area since the parents, invariably, dismiss the whole enquiry as of no significance. In clinical work, however, we see significant preoccupation of children with anal functions. At this stage I would like to mention that the shame–guilt coordinate manifests itself on the basis of modesty training which is more predominant in our culture. The obsessive compulsive phenomena very frequently noted are, to a certain extent, legitimized by religious rituals. The culture also provides modes of 'undoing' which are socially acceptable. For those who do not or cannot utilize these outlets, an overwhelming sense of guilt is the legacy. As Erikson says, 'Naturally, the parental set is at first infantile in nature: the fact that human conscience remains partially infantile throughout life is the core of human tragedy. For the superego of the child can be primitive, cruel and uncompromising, as may be observed in instances where children overcontrol or overconstrict themselves to the point of self-obliteration; where they develop an overt obedience more literal than the one the parent has wished to exact; or where they develop deep regressions and lasting resentments because the parents themselves do not seem to live up to the new conscience which they have instilled in the child.'[9]

The latency period is posing a disturbing dilemma in our clinical work. This is expected to be a phase of 'industry'. After the turbulence of the oedipal phase has been rendered quiescent a child can apply himself to the work world which is the school in this stage. The demands made on the child are so overwhelming that he is denied the sense of accomplishment.

The school system in India is a highly competitive, rigid, unimaginative complex which makes absolutely no allowances for individual variations. The child is adjusted on the basis of certain arbitrarily established criteria of academic competence. The child's worth is assessed on the basis of his school performance. His acceptance by his parents, his status among his siblings, his relationship with his peer group and finally his self-image are all determined on the basis of his performance in school. His individual tastes, his special aptitudes and even his freedom of choice have no meaning. In this situation either he subdues his individuality or falls by the wayside. The results are well known to clinicians. The danger, at this stage, 'lies in a sense of inadequacy and inferiority. If he despairs of his tools and skills or of his status among tool partners his ego boundaries suffer, and he abandons hope for the ability to identify early with others who apply themselves to the same general section of the tool world.'[10]

In our clinical work we repeatedly see children of school age as inhibited and diffident. Their main defence is avoidance. They refuse to perform given tasks. In the psychiatric evaluation, which is relatively unstructured and less demanding, they may relax a little, but in the psychological testing situation they freeze. They perceive testing as an examination and equate the whole set-up with school. We get repeated evidence of distorted perceptions of the environment, confusion as regards status at home and very poor self-image. Under these circumstances one can only speculate about the consequences.

A few comments about youth are now necessary. A young person is, more or less, steered towards a vocation in keeping with his abilities in the external reality. Here we see a paradoxical situation. Those who are guided resent it and those who, for various reasons, have to clear a pathway for themselves remain dissatisfied. The desire, however, is for an understanding person to guide and direct. This is seen in the clinical situation where patients in a subtle way demand guidance and are receptive to suggestions. Even in adults there is almost a nostalgic desire for the approval and sanction of the father at every step. I have seen men of thirty, even fifty, who for all practical purposes are satisfactorily fulfilling adult roles, confessing, in the treatment situation, a dissatisfaction at their competence, as if looking for someone to pat them on the back and tell them that they have done well. Two different factors seem to determine this state of affairs. One situation is where the father has been physically absent from the scene or is not available for close interpersonal interaction. The individual copes with this situation by idealizing the father. It is as if the ghost of the father always hovers around such individuals. Only when this idealization is resolved in the transference situation that there is redemption. In some cases the loss or absence of the father is so poignant that in the treatment situation I accept the role of substitute father and support them. One may question the therapeutic veracity of such a situation, but from experience I have learnt that this allows them to fulfil their life tasks adequately.

An altogether different situation is the one where, in an extended family, the father is present but ineffective. The paternal grandfather is the dynamic head of the family. The father is there almost by default. The confusion this creates has many implications. At an earlier stage the oedipal conflict remains unresolved. The earlier identification patterns are consequently nebulous. During adolescence this manifests itself in many acting out behaviours. At times the negative identification assumes almost psychotic proportions. In treatment sessions, hatred towards the father figure and death wishes are openly expressed. As a nineteen-year-old young man put it, 'Why should I follow my father's advice? He has no guts to separate from my grandfather. I don't respect him.' In these patients the paradigm of the relationship with the mother is very significant. I have repeatedly heard patients say that the mother has played no significant role in their lives. She is perceived as a passive, ineffective person who is also a victim of the father's inadequacy. She needs to be pitied rather than looked up to for support. My earlier comments about her maintenance of role status by manipulation are pertinent here. There is a subtle identification with the mother which further reinforces one's own impotence.

I have deliberately used the term 'impotence' because the whole sexual adjustment in these situations is in the doldrums. In males it is not inadequacy as sexual partners, but more the absence of a total orgiastic experience. To quote Erikson, 'To put it more situationally: the total fact of finding, via the climactic turmoil of the orgasm, a supreme experience of the mutual regulation of two beings in some way takes the edge off the hostilities and potential rages caused by the oppositeness of male and female, of fact and fancy, of love and hate. Satisfactory sex relations make sex less obsessive, overcompensation less necessary, sadistic controls superfluous.'[11] The sexual aspect is a much tabooed subject in our society. We seldom think about it without a sense of guilt. The ideal is abstinence or controlled sex towards the primary goal of procreation. This whole aspect is so unrealistic for the vast majority of people that they constantly live in an unreal world. The only way an individual can cope with it is by having a total split in his value orientation. This is reflected in many young people's failure in a premarital sex experience (which by no means is uncommon, as seen in case history after case history).

On a broader social canvas we have seen a veritable revolt of young people during the past few years, often resulting in violence and meaningless destruction. Albeit many of the methods of expressing dissidence and protest resemble the earlier tested and tried methods during the freedom movement. This similarity, however, is superficial. There is nothing purposive or goal-directed in the current behaviour. There is no ideological base. Most of the time the issues against which protest is going on are so trivial that they would be laughable if they were not so pathetic. In some isolated spots the movement has very clearly defined social goals where narrow interests are totally eschewed. One could almost discern an attempt to establish a positive identity in terms of exposing the hollow ideological fervour of adults and their Janus-faced manifestations. The goals set are realistic and attainable. Unfortunately, such movements fizzle out for lack of mature adult leadership. Indeed, all adult support is suspect and unceremoniously rejected. The movements fail, as they are expected to, since they resemble the characteristic of adolescent temperament lability: a very intense cathexis over a cause or an issue one moment and an indifference towards the same issue the next. It is interesting to note that many manifestations of student and youth protest witnessed in India over the last few years bear a close resemblance to protests staged by the adults against real or imaginary injustices. In western cultures there was an 'establishment' consisting of adults against which youth could revolt. Here, the establishment revolted against the establishment. Some social scientists claim that even though ostensibly the causes for protest were trivial and irrelevant, they were based on frustration resulting from very real injustices. If this is true, why are they not articulated? If the adults are not sensitive to the true nature of these sentiments, whose fault is it? No matter who is to be blamed, the consequences of such actions are, to say the least, disastrous. As Erikson has stated, 'Without some such ideological commitment, however implicit in a "way of life", youth suffers a confusion of values which can be specifically dangerous to some but which on a large scale is surely dangerous to the fabric of society.'[12]

In the clinical set-up we see paradigms of adult failure. In the case illustrations I have presented, the uncertainty, the dependence, and incapacity to make independent decisions are all obvious. These comments are not meant to be denigrating but are in pursuance of my thesis that the social structure does not permit the emergence of a cogent adult role as perceived in western societies. Subordinating one's individual needs to the interests of the group, be it a family, a kinship group, a clan or a class, is upheld as a virtue. The linear structure of authority distribution reinforces and sustains this paradigm. Thus self-assertion becomes selfishness, independent decision making is perceived as disobedience. The response from the in-group is tacit disapproval if not outright condemnation. Under such circumstances it is easier to play safe. The only way this can be accomplished is by passive aggressive behaviour or regression into total passivity. Up to a certain point passivity provides an escape but in the present day and age, life tasks demand a certain assertiveness and some capacity to make decisions. Inability to fulfil these requirements leads to frustration. Inevitably, frustration beyond a point results in ego disintegration in the individual and disorganization in the social structure. As Erikson points out, 'What I mean by this sinister reference is that there is a limit to a child's and an adult's individual endurance in the face of demands which force him to consider himself, his body, his needs, and his wishes as evil and dirty, and to believe in the infallibility of those who pass judgement. Occasionally, he may turn things around, become secretly oblivious to the opinion of others, and consider as evil only the fact that they exist: his chance will come when they are gone or when he can leave them.'[13] The above comments are prompted by the conviction that in India we have to do some fresh thinking about our whole value system. It is not that the traditional beliefs and the values on which they are based are totally irrelevant. These values should be seen in a historical perspective. In an agrarian, relatively less competitive social structure where kinship bonds had economic, social and moral justifications, the value system certainly had a place. In the present day we have to ask if they still fulfil individual and societal needs. The distress caused in individual lives and the fragility of a social structure which can get disorganized at the slightest stress, calls for social scientists to objectively evaluate the present situation. Social scientists must be aware of critical phases in their culture and play an effective role in creating conditions in the socio-cultural milieu conducive to a healthier development of individuals and to maintain the continuity of both the individual and a strong community. It is unpardonable, almost immoral, to ignore the reality of the situation and take recourse to platitudes. Denial of reality is a very poor defence mechanism as we all know. Perhaps the question we have to ask ourselves is: do we understand the reality as it exists today?

NOTES AND REFERENCES

1. Erik H. Erikson, 'Reflections of Dr Borg's Life Cycle', *Daedalus*, 1976, p. 105.
2. Erikson, 'Psychosocial Identity', *International Encyclopedia of Social Sciences*, New York, The Macmillan Company and the Free Press, p. 62.
3. Erikson, 'Identity and The Life Cycle', *Psychological Issues*, No. 1, 1959, p. 123.
4. Ben Schlesinger, 'The Changing Patterns of the Hindu Joint Family System in India', *Marriage and Family Living*, 23, 1961, p. 170.
5. David B. Lynn, 'The Husband–Father Role in the Family', *Marriage and Family Living*, 23, 1961, p. 296.
6. Documentary evidence in support of this thesis is provided by G. M. Carstairs, *The Twice Born*, Bloomington, Indiana University Press, 1958 and B. Whiting (ed.), *Mothers in Six Cultures*, Cambridge, Harvard University Press, 1975.
7. Erikson, *Identity: Youth and Crisis*, London, Faber & Faber, 1968, p. 163.
8. Erikson, 'Psychosocial Identity', op. cit., p. 65.
9. Erikson, *Childhood and Society*, London, Faber & Faber, 1961, p. 225.
10. Ibid., p. 227.
11. Ibid., p. 230.
12. Erikson, *Identity: Youth and Crisis*, p. 188.
13. Ibid., p. 111.

THE YOUNG AND THE OLD

Ambiguity of Role-models and Values among Indian Youth

DURGANAND SINHA

Youth is a distinct and important period in the life cycle of the individual. Sometimes youth has been stereotyped as being rash, indiscreet, impulsive and foolish, and the expression '*gadah pachisi*' ('donkey's twenty-five') is current in some regional languages, characterizing the tendency of youth to resort to unwise and impetuous behaviour which is expected of an individual up to the age of twenty-five and which should be ignored by understanding elders. But in spite of certain derogatory and undesirable features sometimes ascribed to it, in certain respects youth marks the peak in the physical and mental growth of the individual. There are legends and stories in which great kings of yore resorted to penance and worship to maintain the vigour and grandeur of youth eternally, or to regain it after it had been lost with the onset of old age. The period after youth may be characterized by greater wisdom and maturity, but there is a widespread belief that a general decline, however imperceptible and gradual it may be, sets in soon after. Therefore, it is not surprising that youth is not only cherished, but that there is often a yearning in the later years to return to this phase of one's life cycle.

Youth is characterized by a biological 'coming of age'. It ends the period of one's childhood and adolescence, and marks an entry into adulthood. However, psychologically speaking, this period has often been viewed as one of crisis which every individual has to face in varying degrees. It is only by resolving this crisis in some fashion that he can develop emotionally and socially into an adult. This period of crisis, whether it be in the life of an individual or that of a whole generation of young people, is often reflected in certain kinds

of strains and stresses and has been variously described as a generation gap, vocational and social disorientation, alienation, ambiva-
lence and 'identity confusion'. The concept of identity confusion, as
defined by Erikson, denotes a person's uncertainty about his future
role in society, as well as a sense of discontinuity between his personal past and his future.[1] As experienced subjectively, it means a
feeling of fragmentation, of indecision, and of isolation from social
and interpersonal contacts. It is not the purpose of this paper to
elaborate on the concept of identity confusion or its allied concept of
identity crisis. It would be quite sufficient to say that an intensified
form of such confusion is reflected in a variety of psycho-social
disorders such as anxiety, anomie, despair, depersonalization, mean-
inglessness, isolation, loneliness, a feeling of anonymity, and pessi-
mism, all of which seem to characterize contemporary youth.

At certain periods in history, the resolving of identity confusion on
the part of individuals becomes particularly difficult. Certain cultural
and historical factors influence this intensity, and an important one is
the rapidity of change through which a particular society is passing.
One of the features of modern Indian society is the rapid breakdown
of traditional values, and the transitional character of its social,
political and economic structures. This phenomenon of transition
has been taken to underlie the general incidence of high anxiety
which has been observed among the Indian student population.[2]
There have been revolutionary changes in the entire pattern of life
within the last three decades. Old values have tumbled and the new
are still in a state of flux. The phenomenon characterizes most Asian
countries. According to Leon Guerrero, once the Filipino Am-
bassador in London, the elements in all the movements in western
history—the break-up of the Roman Empire, the overthrow of the
feudal system, the Renaissance, the Reformation, the French and
American revolutions, the disruption of the social system in the
industrial revolution, the class-war of the Russian revolution—are
all simultaneously bubbling in the Asian revolution. Gunnar Myrdal
has also commented on this confusing rapidity and disorderly sequence of all-round changes that are taking place in India and other
Asian countries: 'It is, then, not only a telescoping in the sense that
the changes are concentrated in a shorter time span, but there is also
a break in the order in which the changes occur. What could in
Europe unfold gradually and proceed as a grand symphony with one
movement following the other in thematic sequence is by destiny

syncopated in South Asia into almost a cacophony.'[3] In such a period of rapid change, the problem of identity confusion is intensified by the breakdown of traditional values and traditional roles, where adult support for youth's search for identity is lacking and where the guidelines for accepted behaviour get blurred and contradictory. On the plane of individual personality, it is often reflected in the experience of contradictions and inner conflicts, and a mode of life which has been characterized as 'compartmentalization'.[4] While analysing the cultural factors in the emergence of anxiety, I have also remarked on the dichotomies inherent in the Indian situation and personality, and have characterized this as 'tolerance of dissonance'.[5] Nirad Chaudhuri designates it as 'Janus Multifrons', and talks of the 'terrible dichotomy' of Hindu personality with a large number of antithetical though connected traits shaping behaviour. These 'opposites almost neutralize one another, and the indecisive tug-of-war stultifies all his actions.'[6]

Man inherits a limited repertory of responses. Most of the responses are learned, and a majority of them are learned from others, i.e. culturally acquired. In this respect, among other cultural influences, the perception of role-models which the individual tries to emulate and regards as providing guidelines for his conduct, and the perception of what is right and wrong, proper and improper, have a vital part to play in the psychological growth of the individual. The present paper reports the results of a few studies conducted in 1969 and constituting parts of a larger project on intergenerational differences which reflect the ambiguities and confusion of Indian youth today.[7] Directly, this essay is concerned with an analysis of choice of hero-image and role-models, and perception and evaluation of certain 'ambiguous' socio-moral traits as well as of some events and incidents representing transgression of certain accepted codes of behaviour. The strategy of the study was to contrast the reactions of youth against those of persons belonging to the older generation. The sample studied consisted of 300 university and college students from the city of Allahabad, 150 younger teachers below 25, and 150 university and college teachers who were 40 years or above. The overall mean age of the older teachers was 48.18 years, that of younger teachers 23.03, and a little over 19 and 16 years respectively for university and college students.

The sample was subjected to three tests. The first consisted of perception of people and determination of role-models and hero-images. The subject was asked to name five persons from whose life he may have gathered inspiration and who, he considered, had influenced him in his life and behaviour. Later, he was asked to name two of these persons in order, and to indicate the one he regarded as the greatest. Third, he was requested to name the qualities possessed by those two persons which made them notable. An analysis of responses indicated the role-models accepted by the subject as well as the qualities he considered significant.

On the second test, namely, the perception of events, the subject was required to evaluate a number of situations with socio-moral connotations. Each one depicted a transgression of some common social or moral code like misappropriation of public funds because the individual was in urgent need of money; burning of a shop by a crowd because it had not put down its shutters when a general strike was declared; having a secret love-affair with a married woman; travelling without a ticket; and similar other situations. The incidents were chosen to represent some typical, commonplace occurrences. The incidents were presented one by one to the subject, and he was required to indicate whether he considered each 'proper' or 'improper', or whether he was unable to decide about it ('neutral response'). The frequencies of each of the three types of responses were then analysed.

The third study consisted of the presentation of a list of ambiguous behaviour traits as well as other qualities like honesty, cheating, etc. which could be considered desirable or undesirable. A long list containing some desirable, undesirable, and ambiguous behaviour traits, randomly mixed, was presented to the subject and he was asked to indicate whether each quality, when found in a person, would be considered good or bad, positive or negative, desirable or undesirable.

The First Study

The analysis of choice of role-models and heroes revealed interesting age differences. The older generation of teachers displayed a higher degree of agreement among themselves regarding the choice of persons and personalities from whom they received inspiration. They belonged both to the past and the present and constituted figures from the political as well as religious world while some were social reformers. Among the young, both students and teachers, the choice of models was more widely dispersed. It was observed that the hero-image and models for the younger generation were more varied and unstable. Barring outstanding personalities like Mahatma Gandhi, Nehru and Lal Bahadur Shastri, they did not seem to have any clear-cut role-models from whom they derived inspiration and after whom they would like to shape their conduct. The young displayed relatively greater variety in their choice. Apart from the three personalities mentioned earlier, they referred to a large number of figures from the political world, some being quite obscure local personalities, and even film stars and sports champions. It was also observed that all their models belonged to the contemporary world, and that in their choice, there was little general agreement among themselves. Unlike the young, the older sample mentioned even mythological and legendary personalities frequently, and confined their choice generally to well-known mythological, historical, or contemporary people famous for their contributions to the fields of science, literature, politics, religion, and social reform. Lack of agreement and a high degree of diversity in the choice of models reflect uncertainty and instability of role-models for the young. However, it is to be observed that when the subject was asked to indicate the qualities which he thought made those persons great, there was considerable agreement not only among the two groups representing the young, but also between the younger and older generations. The most frequently mentioned qualities were patriotism, statesmanship, humanitarianism, social reform and so on. It may be noted that though these were frequently mentioned by the young as qualities that made their heroes great, many of the heroes chosen (for example, film stars, cricket players, etc.) were such that these qualities could hardly be said to reside in them. This emphasizes further the ambiguity of role-models among the young.

The Second Study

Similar uncertainty and instability was noticed in the analysis of evaluation of incidents representing socio-moral transgressions. It may be mentioned that compared with the older generation, the young displayed a more permissive and less condemnatory stance. This was true for six out of twelve events which were evaluated. However, what was more intriguing was that there was a sizable proportion of uncertain 'neutral' responses to most of these situations. This was particularly high among the two samples representing the young. In other words, when confronted with a socio-moral dilemma, the younger generation displayed considerable hesitation in judging it either as proper or improper, and preferred to suspend judgement. In at least half the incidents presented to them, one-fifth to one-third of the evaluative responses were 'neutral'. The corresponding figures among the older generation of teachers was some ten to fifteen per cent lower. In other words, faced with situations involving socio-moral issues, the younger generation tended to vacillate and suspend judgement more than the older. Thus, youth reflected a comparatively weak super-ego development and a failure to reconcile with the changing moral codes. The net result was a relative lack of certainty about their opinions and judgements. Or, to put it in the words of Nirad Chaudhuri, they were 'torn by their internal psychological tussles'.

The Third Study

On the qualities considered desirable or undesirable in a person it was observed that there was no difference between the young and the old on the so-called 'cardinal virtues' like honesty, duty, non-violence and so on. However, it was observed that there was greater agreement regarding the importance of these among the two groups belonging to the same generation than between the groups representing different generations. Further, such a concurrence was small regarding qualities which were considered undesirable in a person. While the younger teachers and students agreed among themselves regarding qualities considered undesirable (correlation being 0.88), there was only moderate agreement between the young and the old (correlation being 0.49 between older teachers and students, and 0.48 between older teachers and young teachers).

On another measure, the difference between the young and the old was reflected in the perception and evaluation of some 'ambiguous' traits. During pre-testing, twelve behaviour traits were found to yield 'ambiguous' responses, i.e. these traits were such that they had almost equal probability of being judged as either desirable or undesirable in a person. On these behaviour traits differences were observed between the generations. Evaluation of some of these behaviour traits among the young and the old was divergent. With regard to some, like cunning (*chalak*), opportunist (*avsarvadi*) and the like, the young tended to regard them more frequently as 'desirable', while the older generation viewed them as 'undesirable'. The case was similar with qualities like sentimental (*bhavuk*) and restless (*chanchal*) where the differences were in the reverse direction. In other words, such evaluative differences of a few so-called 'ambiguous' behaviour traits were indicative of the divergence in values. Further, such differences in perception made it difficult for the young to adopt and accept the members of the older generation as their model.

Conclusion

The above findings illustrate a number of points. There is a value ambiguity among the young, as a result of which they are not able to have clear-cut evaluative responses to certain socio-moral issues. This ambiguity reflects a socio-moral dilemma faced by them and a vacillation and uncertainty characterizing their handling of such situations.

The reason for this ambiguity in the young can only be guessed. One of the factors which is likely to be operating is the relative lack of exposure in the older generation to mass media while the younger generation is almost completely immersed in various mass media like radio, films, television, the press, and magazines so that the world of arts, sports, entertainment and contemporary events are constantly brought within their psychological field, leading to a proliferation of role-models available to them. While the choice of the older generation was largely limited to the figures and personalities about whom they had heard from their elders in the form of stories and legends or read in books which projected more or less unambiguous roles for them, the young are confronted with a large array of 'not-so-important' figures that have been made familiar to them by the mass media. As a result, the young have available to them a wide range of models for making their choice. The proliferation of roles with which they are confronted, make it difficult for them to identify completely with any set of clear-cut roles or personalities, which is important in the formation of ego-identity. This is reflected in the fact that, barring a few exceptions, the frequencies of choice in selecting a particular figure as a hero was relatively low in the younger group. Since heroes for the contemporary generation were diverse, mostly consisting of minor personalities, it can be asserted that by and large there was an absence of what may be called normative models for the youth as a group. While the outstanding heroes could provide definite roles, the roles tended to get largely obscured in the person of minor heroes.

The young very rarely found their identification models among the great personalities of the past. This is indicative of the absence of a link with the past and with traditional values. A mature psychological identity presupposes a subjective sense of continuous existence, and a coherent memory. It is anchored in the past and at the same time links itself to the future. This continuity did not seem to exist in the case of the young.

It is often suggested that in the process of identity formation the individual looks to some persons, usually parents, teachers, elders or someone from his peer group, whom he tries to emulate and whose qualities he tries to introject into himself. They provide him with guidelines for conduct and help him in resolving identity confusion. But the sample of youth studied seldom found inspiration from personalities from the past, and also very rarely chose their parents or teachers as their role-models. The reason for this is not hard to find. It is quite likely that for the bulk of the rural youth who had 'migrated' from the villages to the university or the colleges with new aspirations and professional goals, the values and life-patterns represented by their parents, had very little worth emulating. Once they had shifted to the cities, they were completely overwhelmed by the pattern of life, the new norms prevalent on the campuses, and were dazzled by the new values. Parents in some cases may have been the focus of identification earlier, but at least at this stage they had ceased to play any significant role in providing models for conduct and life-goals to the younger generation.

A similar attitude is fostered by the students towards their teachers, which is indicative of the psychological distance between the two groups. A general attitude of hostility towards teachers has lately developed in many educational institutions. Whatever the reason for this rejection, the diversity and uncertainty of the response of youth indicate that they not only reject the past but also their parents and teachers. These have not been replaced by other stable models, so that as a group the young do not possess clear-cut role-models, which makes the resolution of identity confusion more difficult.

It is further observed that the elders who could constitute the role-models for the young are themselves often perceived as presenting an ambiguous façade. It is suggested that the elders of today when they were themselves young could easily identify and find role-models among the older generation of that time because the latter belonged to a more stable society and presented figures which were not torn by contradictions. But this is no longer the case with contemporary youth. Due to value contradictions and conflicts which have beset them in a fast changing world, the older generation of today, who could have provided guidelines of conduct, have in their own lives failed to provide stable models free from ambiguity and contradictions.[8] It is felt that the consequent role-ambiguity and ambiguity of values which confront the youth have intensified the problem of resolution of identity confusion. It shows itself in a kind of 'role refusal' on the part of the young, and is reflected in unrest on the campuses, the development of a 'counter culture', and intergenerational differences which is creating tension in many spheres of India's social life. The absence of ideological commitment, which seems to characterize youth on many campuses, further complicates the problem of identity formation.

NOTES AND REFERENCES

1. E. H. Erikson, *Identity: Youth and Crisis*, New York, W. W. Norton and Co., 1968, p. 87.
2. D. Sinha, 'Cultural factors in the emergence of anxiety', *Eastern Anthropologist*, 25(1), 1962, pp. 21–37.
3. G. Myrdal, *Asian Drama: An Enquiry into the Poverty of Nations*, vol. I, New York, Pantheon, 1968, pp. 119–20.
4. J. L. M. Dawson, 'Traditional values and work efficiency in a West African mine labour force', *Occupational Psychology*, 37, 1963, pp. 209–18.
5. D. Sinha, 'Indian personality and motivation in the context of economic development', paper presented during the International Congress of Applied Psychology, Montreal, 1974.
6. N. Chaudhuri, *The Continent of Circe*, Bombay, Jaico Publishing House, 1966, p. 106.
7. For a complete report see D. Sinha, *The Mughal Syndrome: A Psychological Study of Intergenerational Differences*, New Delhi, Tata McGraw-Hill, 1972.
8. I have analysed this point at some length in an earlier paper and have regarded it as one of the factors generating high anxiety among modern youth. See my 'Cultural factors in the emergence of anxiety', op. cit.

5

PASSAGE TO ADULTHOOD

Perceptions from Below

S. K. THORAT

In these pages I shall try to explore some aspects of identity and adulthood in Indian society. Having been born a Mahar, I bring to these issues a perspective shaped in the ranks of the lower castes in a Maharashtrian village. The discussion will centre on my personal experiences and observations, and it will make some reference to writings that I have read.

Let me begin with a brief summary of the social position of the untouchables. Nearly every village in India has its untouchables, and their social and economic positions have been uniformly low. In the 1971 census they accounted for fifteen per cent of India's population; of this, nearly seven-eighths lived in villages and about one-eighth in urban areas. India's overall level of urbanization is twenty per cent, so the scheduled castes have been disproportionately rural. In the migration from rural to urban areas, they have been participating less than the upper castes; and Victor D'Souza has attributed this to the difficulty which the scheduled castes—lacking a comparable social and economic base—have in competing with the upper castes for the more rewarding urban work opportunities. Hence their growing concentration in rural areas, and their growing dependence on the upper caste landowners in villages.

In addition to social discrimination, the untouchables are also subject to economic exploitation by the caste Hindus.

In Maharashtra, the scheduled castes constituted 5.63 per cent of the population in 1961. If the scheduled castes who have been converted to Buddhism are added, they would constitute about 14 per cent of the population. The principal scheduled castes in Maharashtra are: Mahar, 35.12 per cent, Mang, 32.65 per cent and Chambhar 22.06 per cent. These three castes account for nearly 90 per cent of the total. Castes called Bhangi, Dhor, and Molar account for most of the others.

Noteworthy in the Maharashtrian scene has been the conversion of scheduled castes to Buddhism. In 1961, Maharashtra had 27.90 lakh Buddhists who constituted 85 per cent of the total Buddhist population of India and 7.05 per cent of the State's total population. A majority of the Buddhists are from the Mahar community, about half of whom have been converted to Buddhism.

I shall approach the question of identity and adulthood against this background. I find useful the following definition of identity:

those points of reference whereby persons (or a group) define themselves in relation to the world and to other people: an awareness of persons (or a group) of who they are and where they belong. . . . the problem of identity has another dimension. It is related to the sense of group solidarity in the acceptance of certain values, goals, or meanings.[2]

While this general definition of identity is useful, the identity of the untouchables has been shaped by a range of socially imposed disabilities; it belongs to the category defined by Berreman as 'stigmatized ethnic identity':

First, that stigmatized ethnic identity is experienced as oppression. It is a human day-to-day experience of degradation and exploitation, not simply an abstract concept.

Second, that people resent that identity and that experience regardless of the rationalizations offered for it.

Third, that people continually attempt to resist, escape, alleviate or change that identity and that experience. . . .

Fourth, how people respond to stigamatized ethnic identity depends upon their definitions of themselves, of others, and of the situations in which they interact.

Mencher continues the quotation from Berreman:

. . . it is not consensus on the legitimacy of systems of oppression which enables them to continue, but agreement on who has the power, and when and under what circumstances and with what effect it is likely to be used. . . . People cease to get along in stratified societies when *this* crucial agreement changes or is challenged. . . . resistance to stigmatized ethnic identity . . . is an intrinsic and inescapable feature of systems incorporating such identity. . . .

In the light of the foregoing, I propose to discuss some aspects of the identity of untouchable adults, relying especially on my own experience.

An untouchable child, particularly in a village, is subjected to a stigmatized identity from the time he can begin to walk and to touch things and people. When he innocently enters the village temple or a caste Hindu household, or touches someone, he is reprimanded either by his parents or by the caste Hindus. Although he would have been identified even earlier as a child of an untouchable father, this would not have affected his thinking process directly. It is when he begins to walk independently, and when the play of his own will takes him to other people and things, that he experiences a stigmatized identity personally; and this makes an impression, subtle and indirect, upon his thinking process. This is also the period when his family members or caste-mates, or the caste Hindus, begin to make him aware of the particular limits to the range of his social contacts.

The growing child continues to receive this guidance until such time as he comes to understand his stigmatized identity himself. Later, as an adult, he may either accept or reject this identity, or do both partially. For the development of the untouchable child, then, this period between his beginning to walk independently and his adulthood is crucial, for during this period he experiences the stigma repeatedly attached to him and, correspondingly, he receives—from his parents or others—explanations justifying or questioning the bases of his stigma. It is this chain of experiences and explanations over a period of time that gives shape to the personality of the adult and to his attitudes towards his stigmatized identity. It is the balance between these experiences and explanations that leads him to either reject or accept that identity.

To illustrate, suppose a child is admonished for having touched a temple or a person from the higher castes. If his parents or relatives respond submissively by telling him that he should not have done the touching since he is an untouchable, he would also accept the idea. If such experiences continue consistently over time, the child would accept his stigma without question. But if his father objects to the admonition, quarrels with caste Hindus by saying, 'If we are untouchable, so what? We have a right to enter the village temple or use the common well,' this would stimulate the child to think, and whenever he faces such discrimination and finds his parents responding in this manner, he would go on developing an attitude of rejection towards his stigmatized identity.

His attitude towards his stigmatized identity during adulthood would be shaped by many forces. By now he is aware of the meaning and the nature of his stigma. He is aware of the fact that he is untouchable in the eyes of caste Hindus and is expected to behave in a particular way towards them. Whether he accepts or rejects this stigmatized identity will depend on many forces around him, such as:

—the explanations given to him by his parents, caste-mates, and caste Hindus, defending or challenging the stigma.
—the social trends around him, that is, whether or not there is a social struggle against untouchability and the caste system.
—his education and the general educational level in the community.
—the type of education, whether or not it supports, directly or indirectly, the present social structure.
—his experiences in school and in other groups.
—the kind of social and religious ideologies he may have encountered and, perhaps, accepted.

I proceed now to consider some personal experiences and observations. I shall discuss particularly the nature of the stigma experienced and my reactions to it, changes in the content of the stigma, my tendency to reject the identity altogether, and then an attempt to create a new identity and its content. In these experiences, my family had a vital role, for the attitudes of my close kinsmen influenced my perceptions of the inequalities directly; the social awareness thus generated produced in me a desire for education, and for this education I received varied and unfailing support from my family. In turn, this education improved my understanding of the nature of social inequality. I can discuss these related issues in four broad phases:

Acceptance: from one to ten years.
Rejection of stigmatized identity: from ten to sixteen years.
Forming a new identity: from sixteen to twenty-two years.
Outgrowing my caste's boundaries.

Acceptance: from one to ten years

In village society an untouchable child is identified on the basis of his caste by caste Hindus, including his friends among them. His caste identity is the very first for the child. It is not passive or abstract; it has an active element of social degradation. I remember, for example, that whenever I happened to walk through a caste Hindu locality, the caste Hindus would identify me as a 'son of Kasanya Mahar'. This identification was doubly disparaging: it an-

nounced my membership in an untouchable caste, and it employed a
rude form of my father's name, Kisan.

Humiliation in the village could take many forms. Once while I
was playing with a ball, it went near the village well. In picking up
the ball, I happened to touch the well. Noticing this, the son of the
Patel, the village headman, grabbed me by the neck and slapped me.
My mother intervened and asked for forgiveness, for I was an innocent child. She warned me immediately that we were Mahars and
not expected to touch the village well. On many other occasions when
I happened to touch things in the homes of some high caste families,
my mother would direct me not to touch things or people there. I
simply accepted this.

My tendencies at this time were undoubtedly influenced by the
religious atmosphere in my family, although the extent of religious
involvement varied from one person to another. My mother was,
and continues to be, most religious. At each ceremony she would
ask me to bow my head before the family deity, and I would do so;
in early childhood I did not think of objecting. My father's only
religious practice was to bow to the sun, *suryanamaskar*, every
morning; he observed no other ritual.

My eldest brother came to be involved in religious activity as he
could read the *Mahabharata*, *Ramayana*, *Gita*, and other Hindu
religious books; and because of his knowledge of Hindu religion,
and also his interest in music and singing, he was asked to participate
in the high caste Hindu Bhajan Mandal in the temple. Every evening
the village had community religious singing at the village temple,
when men of scheduled castes took the lead and played the instruments. The Maratha and other high castes joined in it. My brother
became an active singer in this group. I used to be keen to participate
in the singing also and to be allowed free access to the temple, but
high caste participants would tell me to sit apart, not to enter the
sanctum, and not to touch the image of the deity. Partly because of
the involvement of my mother and my eldest brother, I was keen to
participate in the religious activity, to do things as the high castes
did them; but in later years, as I shall show below, I broke with this
whole complex of activities. My middle brother, fourteen or fifteen
years old at this time, was not at all religious and would oppose all
religious observances in the family.

As I think back over this period, I find that as an immature child
I used to accept the stigmatized identity for the simple reason that

I did not have the capacity to raise questions concerning it; but between 1955 and 1957, while I went to primary school, aged six to eight years, I was already surrounded by the social movement prevailing all over Maharashtra, although I did not understand its significance. The movement reached a peak during 1957 when I was in the third standard, aged eight. Because of this movement I had many experiences in the village that made it possible for me to question my identity in later years. I shall now recount some of these experiences to illustrate the social ferment in the village in those years.

In response to Ambedkar's call, when many of the Mahars in the village took to Buddhism in 1956, they also stopped eating beef and carrion and left their traditional village occupations, like carrying away dead animals. Consequently, the upper castes in the village subjected them to a social and economic boycott, denying them employment for two months, preventing their entry into village shops, etc. Some of the untouchable labourers, then, would go to a nearby village for labour. Later the upper castes realized that they could not do their agricultural work without untouchable labourers, and they lifted their boycott.

The untouchables were threatened physically too. In response, the untouchables established a village branch of a much wider militant movement initiated by Ambedkar, namely the Samta Sainik Dal, a 'corps for social equality'. Its task was to fight against the social injustice done to the untouchables by the upper castes. Its members also acted as volunteers, helping in the organization of large meetings and protecting their leaders. Young and old, all were its members. The younger members especially were taught to wield wooden staffs, the *lathi*, and other instruments, as if in play. This activity helped create tremendous enthusiasm and self-confidence. My middle brother was an active and militant member, very skilful with the *lathi*, and greatly praised by my father and other people. I was much inspired by him and, in order to participate in this training, I would run away from the night study rooms operated by the school. I enjoyed the activity, but its purpose I did not know then.

The untouchables stopped going to the Hindu temple and they formed their own Bhajan Mandal, called the Jai Bhim Mandal.* They would sing the songs composed by Dinbandhu Segoankar,

---

* Bhim was the first name of Dr B. R. Ambedkar.

Waman Kardak and other contemporary untouchable revolutionary poets. They had, also, a *Kala-pathak*—a folk drama troupe—which dramatized the social disabilities to which we were subject and warned us to fight against them. These plays would affect the untouchables powerfully.

During this period we often had visits from R. S. Gavi, a prominent untouchable leader who supported Ambedkar's ideas. He would deliver speeches in the village. The untouchables were able to start using the village well only in 1953 or 1954, when I was in the second standard. This happened at a function, in the presence of policemen, and Gavi made a powerful speech which I remember. At that time I was the first child to use the village well, and the event encouraged us greatly.

Another important event which affected me directly concerned my immediate family. In 1956 a majority of Mahar untouchables left Hinduism and became Buddhists. Along with others from my village, my father and eldest brother too attended the conversion ceremony. I observed that, after these two had embraced Buddhism, my middle brother took some small copper statues of gods, which my mother worshipped, and had these converted into a small instrument used during bhajans. My mother was very angry with him and would not give him food in the house for some eight or ten days thereafter (our neighbours had to feed him). Subsequently, there was much conflict between my mother and my brother over religious observances, and the religious atmosphere in our family was greatly disturbed. My middle brother stopped beef-eating in our house also and, along with others, he stopped the person who used to bring beef for sale to the village from coming there. (I should note that Ambedkar had urged the stopping of only carrion-eating, but many people went on to oppose beef-eating also. This swing has in recent years been reversed.) He also beat up some caste Hindus because they observed untouchability.

Such was the social milieu in my family and my village while I was growing up. It created many impressions on my mind. In the village it was a period of revolt by the untouchables against social injustice, and it influenced my ideas about social problems. When in later years my understanding grew, I could begin to see the meaning of these past activities. My experiences in the village gave me a sense of conflict, of militancy, and of rejection and, later, I would try to understand the social problems; but perhaps I would not have done this with the same intensity and force if I had not been brought up in such a social atmosphere.

It may be appropriate to digress here to consider the context in which I had my education. Even in 1953, when I began school, it was remarkable for an untouchable child to be sent to school, especially so in a remote village. For the parents it meant an important change because untouchables had been debarred from education for millennia. In sending a son to school the father would, for the first time, be thinking in terms of the future. In families of landless labourers especially, the child is an asset, able to contribute to the family's small income even with his modest labour. In sending such a son to school, his father foregoes the child's contribution.

Many untouchables, and particularly the Mahars, had been wanting to educate their children; and this urge can be traced to the exhortations of Dr B. R. Ambedkar who asked his followers not only to leave their traditional occupations but also to take to education. 'Educate, organize, and agitate'—this was his famous slogan. To act on this urge one needed reasonably easy access to a school, however, and in our village a school was established only in the early 1950s. My elder brothers had wanted to go to school but my father had asked them to work for the family instead, after the second standard, because of poverty in the family. One of my brothers used to and continues to blame my father for denying him an education; and my father too mentions this often and feels very bad about it. In my case my father perhaps felt that he should at least send his last son to school. Also, by the time I began school, my family's economic position had improved somewhat, especially since my two elder brothers were helping to support the family. I should note also that my father owns four acres of dry land, and therefore we were economically better placed than our landless caste-mates.

I was admitted into the first standard when I was five years old, a year below the minimum age, but the school teacher was keen on getting more students into the school. Mine was the second batch of untouchables to go to school in our village—there had been five or six boys in the first batch.

How anxious my parents were for my education was evident in a number of events. In my fifth standard I was admitted to a Christian school and hostel in a village about fifteen miles from my home. Owing to difficulties with the hostel food and the discipline there I was often taken ill, and once during an illness my father brought me home to rest for some days. I was happy enough to miss school, but my father sent me back to school when I recovered, much against my will. On other occasions also he insisted on my continuing with my education.

Since I could not adjust to the hostel atmosphere, I was transferred to another school about six miles from my home. I used to walk there every day with my friends. In the sixth standard we had a teacher from the Chambhar caste who was very concerned about our education; he used to inform our parents about our studies or irregularity in school. Under his guidance I secured the third place in my class.

I remember an incident involving my mother at about this time. I shared a bed with my mother, and kept a hurricane lamp nearby. Sometimes I would go to sleep, with the lamp still burning. One night somehow the lamp overturned, and my mother's sari caught fire, but she was able to bring it under control soon. However, she did not tell me about the incident, lest I feel guilty and stop studying. Later, when I came to know about it I felt very ashamed and stopped reading in bed. The incident revealed my mother's innocent but strong feelings about my studies.

In the eighth standard I was again admitted to a Christian hostel where they provided all one's needs—food, oil, soap, books, etc.— for eight rupees, so that it was almost a free hostel. Every boy had to work in the fields every day, however, and since I could not cope with this work, I left the hostel after two or three months. For the rest of the year I stayed with my mother in a relative's house. My mother used to work in the fields and, with some help from my father, used to provide for us both. That year she made every effort to enable me to continue my studies.

For standards nine and ten I was again admitted to a Christian hostel in Amravati, the district town. By then I had become aware of my parents' struggles, and so I was more serious about my education. In the hostel the food was bad, but I accepted it and continued to study. My father used to come to see me. He would be surprised over the quality of food and my adjustment to it. He would feel very bad about it and would appreciate my effort. I stayed in that hostel half-way through the tenth standard until I was driven out because I did not accept the authorities' suggestion that I become a Christian. I declined this suggestion because I had grown up under Buddhist influence and therefore could not accept the existence of God, nor accept their prayers or religious beliefs. In fact I used to ask the Catholic priest about the existence of God and would be unhappy with his explanation. Some of the younger priests in the hostel were also sexually lax. So I left the hostel and, for two months, rented a room with a friend.

I must say, however, that in my region, and in Maharashtra generally, Christian missionaries have played a crucial role in the untouchables' education at the middle and high school levels. Without their institutions, a majority of untouchables during this period would not have had this education. The missionaries' stress upon equality in social behaviour, upon the untouchables' full right to participate in religious activity, and upon favourable economic arrangements, all these helped to attract untouchable students to them.

Rejection of stigmatized identity: from ten to sixteen years

During this period I was in school from the sixth to the eleventh standard. By then I had learned that I was untouchable by caste and therefore was not allowed into the village temple, the caste Hindu homes, or into the common village dinner. Aware of the limits on my social relations, I used to try to stay within these limits; but whenever subjected to discrimination, I used to oppose it. This reaction to the stigmatized identity was associated with a conscious desire for equal treatment. The reaction was mainly emotional: I would either scold the caste Hindu or develop feelings of hatred. These feelings had no ideological base. I simply thought that I should not be discriminated against; but I was not very clear about the kind of identity I wanted.

Let me illustrate. When I was in the sixth standard, our headmaster invited all the students to dinner. After all of us had sat down, one caste Hindu student had not yet found a place. A place was vacant next to me. The headmaster asked him to sit next to me, but the boy refused, for I was untouchable. I found this to be quite humiliating. On our way back from the dinner, my brother and I beat this student up. This is how I expressed my reaction; I simply thought that he should not have behaved like that. In the evening that day the caste Hindu boy's parents came to our house for a quarrel, but my middle brother drove them away and protected me. This incident inspired me and encouraged me to fight whenever an occasion arose.

When I was in the ninth class, the daughter of the village *Sarpanch* was married. The entire village, including the untouchables, was invited to a dinner at his house. My family went also, and they pressed me hard to join them. I knew, however, that people of scheduled castes had been asked to bring their own glass for drinking water and would be seated apart from the upper castes, and therefore I refused to go. The *Sarpanch* himself came to our house looking for me. I had to evade him because I could not say no to his face. So normally I tried to avoid such situations; and if in spite of this I happened to face discrimination, I would oppose it in one or another form.

In sum, during this period I resisted the stigmatized identity steadily. Yet I was not aware of the type of identity I wanted. I only felt that I should not be subjected to discrimination. During this period I sought also to maintain a certain distance deliberately from caste Hindus. Often I felt ashamed about the submissive attitude of my kinsmen, and then I would maintain a distance from them also.

Forming a new identity: from sixteen to twenty-two years

An uncle of mine was a student in Milind College of Arts, Aurangabad, which had been established by Dr Ambedkar. I used to read the college magazine and had developed a desire to enroll in the college after matriculation, especially because I had been drawn to Dr Ambedkar for many years. So, after passing the matriculation examination, I went to Aurangabad, some three or four hundred kilometres from my village and, with my uncle's help, enrolled in Milind College. I shall return to the special qualities of this college shortly.

During my four years in college my father provided for me, despite all difficulties, though my middle brother, by then employed in Jabalpur (M.P.), would also send some money. To provide for me, my father often had to borrow from a moneylender, at a high rate of interest, but he never refused to meet my needs. Since my father is a very sincere man, he could borrow without difficulty. His friends used to appreciate his efforts for my education and would praise him about my success; this encouraged him to do more for me. I found that he was a very determined person, never discouraged by even very difficult situations. Aware of his devotion, I was very serious in my studies. During my first three years in college I stayed away from all extra-curricular activities—drama, travel, etc.—aiming simply at graduation to begin with.

During my first year in college my mother became mentally very disturbed—and still continues to be so, though she has improved somewhat. Whenever I went home subsequently, my father and I had to share the cooking and other housework. So my father asked me to go to my brother in Jabalpur for summer vacations, where I would get some good food and new clothes. Briefly, during these years I was on my own in academic matters, but my father tried very hard to help me financially. His only motive seemed to be that his last son should get an education.

It was during this period that I received the ideological base and I tried to formulate a new identity. I shall discuss this phase in three parts:

> Foundation of new ideological base
> Formation of new identity
> Activities associated with new identity.

Foundation of new ideological base

As I noted earlier, my opposition to the stigmatized identity had earlier been based only on emotion. After completing my high school, I entered college with many questions in mind. Ninety per cent of the students in Milind College are from the lower castes and they receive every type of social education there, directly or indirectly. It was in this atmosphere of social education and awareness that I was able to develop a new ideological base and a new identity to match it. The process was spread over the four years I spent in the college. I shall now discuss the various facets of life in this college which contributed to the students' social education.

A majority of the students in this college come from backward classes, and they share a more or less similar socio-economic background. In the package of experiences they bring with them, there are many common elements, and they discuss these with each other. This constant articulation of their experiences, and reflection upon them, helps the students see their social problem more clearly; and it stimulates them to try to analyse it and to seek remedies for it.

The college authorities too seek to promote such awareness in more deliberate ways. The attempt is to make the students express themselves: they are made to write out their personal experiences, poems, short stories, essays, drama, etc.; to read out poems and short stories; to make speeches and participate in debates, and so forth. Speeches by outside speakers on social problems are also arranged. The topics of these writings and speeches are centred on social problems like caste and untouchability.

Then there is the study of Buddhist philosophy and Pali language. Students are generally attracted by the opposition of Buddhist philosophy to caste and untouchability, to the *karma* theory based on past deeds, to the theory of reincarnation; by its attack on the entire system of ritualism and blind faith; and by its acceptance of social equality, justice and fraternity. It should be remembered that what the students from backward classes find interesting in Buddhism is its social teaching, not its metaphysics and other abstract issues.

Apart from this subject, the college runs a Buddhist Centre also. It has an extensive programme of lectures, discussions, and celebrations concerning Buddhist teaching for college students, and this leads up to an examination. This is a major activity wherein a student develops his understanding of social problems.

Let me now explain my involvement with this complex of activities. I remember that during my first two years there I was not very active or responsive, but I attended the debating competitions and the speeches on social problems. This inspired me to read and to speak about them. During the last two years my understanding of social problems grew considerably. I came in contact with Buddhist social philosophy through a friend who was a student of Buddhist philosophy and Pali linguistics. I passed two examinations in Buddhist social philosophy. I also read the books of B. R. Ambedkar. I studied the questions of caste, untouchability, and Hinduism, and I learned the bases of the stigmatized identity which I had been subjected to. Hitherto emotional, my opposition now acquired a firm ideological base.

During this period I was continuously rejecting the Hindu social philosophy. I would criticize caste, untouchability, the basic theory of Hinduism—that is, the theory of *karma* based on past deeds, of reincarnation of the eternal soul, of the divine origin of castes and of untouchability, of God, etc.—and all ritualism and blind belief. With the help of this base I started also to write and to deliver speeches against social injustice.

My understanding of social problems was also helped by the study of sociology, one of my subjects, where I studied the question of caste and untouchability with great interest.

I took part in some competitions also. The topics of two of them were, 'Cooperation and the backward classes' and 'Democracy and the caste system'. Participating in them was not a mere matter of form; I had an inner desire to express my views on the problem.

Formation of new identity

Apart from theoretically rejecting the stigmatized identity, during this period I tried also to create a new one. I tried to do this deliberately. Rejecting the old identity and accepting a new one required that there be certain changes in one's way of life, values, social relations, associations with new groups, life style, etc. The new identity should be reflected in these changes. Rejection of the stigmatized identity was through the following:

—I accepted the principles of social justice, equality, fraternity, and the like.
—I rejected belief in the *karma* theory based on past deeds, reincarnation of souls, in God and rituals. I discarded the theory of the divine origin of castes and untouchability and other such Hindu theories based on speculation and belief.
—This was reflected in practice. I refused to celebrate Hindu festivals.
—I dissociated myself from all Hindu religious events in village society, such as entering a temple, going to a village dinner, or participating in the village bhajan group.
—I also discarded beef-eating which was held to be the basis for untouchability.
—I would not go to a caste Hindu home where there was any chance of discrimination.
—I rejected the Hindu ceremony of marriage.

In this third phase, then, I tried to discard the earlier stigmatized identity and to develop a new one based on a different way of life, values, and associations. The entire motive for these changes was drawn from a desire for social equality and for the right social intercourse. I should specifically mention the tremendous mental change that I had undergone. As I mentioned earlier, during the second phase, my opposition to discrimination was largely emotional, but it had another feature also: I was often not very confident about my actions. I used to feel that my feelings were partly right and partly wrong. When, for example, I avoided the dinner at the *Sarpanch's* house, I was sure that I did not want to go, still I felt that there might be something wrong in refusing to join when the entire village was participating. This definite but uncertain state of mind was due to the fact that I did not understand the social questions in their entirety. After studying Buddhist social teaching and Ambedkar's thoughts over the next four or five years, however, I became very firm about my stand and my actions. Now I understood issues which, earlier, had been discussed by R. S. Gavi and others in speeches which I had sometimes found confusing. In similar situations later on, I could argue openly and confidently about the correctness of my stand and could indeed try to persuade others to act similarly. This was a major change in the way my mind worked. I had firmly accepted the ideas of social equality and justice. These came then to be reflected in different forms of social behaviour.

Activities associated with new identity

I stayed out of village activities controlled by caste Hindus, like feasts given by them or the festivals or bhajans organized by them. On the other hand, identifying myself with Buddhist social philosophy and way of life, based on social equality, I began to celebrate the Bhim and Buddha Jayantis, and the anniversary of the famous conversions to Buddhism in 1956, where I would deliver speeches criticizing the Hindu social system. Initially it was the social movement in the village which had given me some sense of my relationship with society. But now during my visits home people would ask about Buddhism and about the wider context of Ambedkar's movement. In my family my brothers asked me many questions about caste, untouchability and Buddhism. The movement had now given way to socio-religious calm, and people looked up to me as an adviser. I used to propagate the ideas of social equality whenever there was an occasion. For example, during my summer visits to my elder brother in Jabalpur, on the occasion of Buddha Jayanti I delivered speeches there. These various activities led me to terminate relations with people and groups who believed in and practised untouchability and to establish active relations with groups that accepted social equality and justice, both in principle and in practice. I could continue this activity in the village so long as I was in college and university; later I tended to lose contact with the village.

Outgrowing my caste's boundaries

This phase covers my two years in post-graduate studies and the three years since then. During this period I became socially and politically active and began to enter into relationships with the caste Hindu social reformers.

During my two years of post-graduate studies at the Marathwada University during 1970–1, my understanding about social problems continued to increase, and I got into more activities. With my friends I formed a Depressed Students Association in Aurangabad where the University is. Within and outside this Association, I participated in morchas, joined discussions, gave speeches, and wrote articles. Such participation still continues.

The important change in my attitudes and activities during this period was that previously I had limited my relations to my own caste people whose social attitudes were similar to mine. At the University and later, however, I came into contact with caste Hindus who really wanted social change and worked for it. I came to be closely associated with such groups. My relations thus crossed the caste boundary and I developed confidence in caste Hindu reformers. My tendency is to associate with people who believe in and practise social equality, regardless of their economic position or political beliefs.

Any untouchable adult is subject to stigmatized identity. Since this is not an abstract thing but a matter of day-to-day oppression and exploitation, educated adults always try to discard it and to accept another identity based on justice and on right social intercourse. I have described my own experience. I came especially under the influence of Dr Ambedkar's social movement, Buddhist philosophy, and rationalist thought. So I tried to form a new identity based on a new self-image; but any educated adult from this background in Maharashtra, whether influenced by Ambedkar's movement or by Marxist thought or by a rationalist outlook through education, has a clear tendency to discard his stigmatized identity and to accept a new one.

What then is the meaning of identity to an untouchable adult? I think the new identity an untouchable adult seeks is in the form of adopting new values, norms, goals, new associations and all that promotes just and right social relations, which in turn would give him social and cultural equality and due social respect. His opposition is not merely to the caste system and the practice of untouchability but to the entire Hindu philosophy which supports social inequality and injustice, along with practices which perpetuate hatred, blind faith, and ignorance. He opposes the entire set of principles and practices which divide society into so many different compartments, so many 'different rat holes', in Ambedkar's words. He wants a new life based on equality, justice, and fraternity, and that requires a complete change in outlook and attitudes towards men and things. So the untouchables want that the entire Hindu social structure, based on injustice, inequality, hatred, and ignorance, should be replaced by one based on social equality, justice, love, fraternity, and a rational outlook. At the end I would say that the caste system (and its reflection, untouchability), with thousands of subcastes, is like so many stinking ponds which have polluted life for all those who came in contact with them. What we want is a flowing river with fresh and pure water.

NOTES AND REFERENCES

1. Victor D'Souza, 'Scheduled castes and urbanization in Punjab: an explanation', *Sociological Bulletin*, 34, 1975, pp. 1–12.
2. Joan Mencher, 'Group and self-identification: the view from the bottom', *ICSSR Research Abstracts Quarterly*, vol. 3, p. 176. The later citation from Gerald Berreman is also used by Mencher in the same paper.

6

A COMMENT ON
'PASSAGE TO ADULTHOOD'

SATISH SABERWAL

Having had a hand in helping Mr Thorat develop his sensitive essay,
I may be allowed to sketch in some of the wider issues which bear
upon his themes. I shall refer particularly (1) to some of the historical
antecedents of the upsurge which engages Thorat's attention; (2) to
the question of how difficult it would generally be for an untouchable
to move out of the caste system in a village and into the larger
modern urban framework of occupations today; and (3) to the
overall, historically conditioned, structural constraints which make
it difficult for the untouchables, and other lowly groups, to mobilize
politically, and otherwise, in defence of their own interests.

1

Among the most insightful elements in Erikson's approach to the
human psyche is the recognition that individual behaviour at any
time reflects, simultaneously, the *historical* heritage of his society and
culture, the course of his own *mental* development, and his functioning as a *biological* organism.[1] The phases which Thorat has used to
organize his account refer to his own bio-psychological maturation,
and these call for no further comment; but I would like to indicate
here how their historical context could be usefully expanded.

Thorat is, of course, aware of his own historical context, and he is
more aware of its depth than his essay shows; but this awareness is
still partial. He concentrates on the social upsurge among the
scheduled castes, inspired by Ambedkar, an upsurge felt all over
India, and enacted with particular intensity among the Mahars of
Maharashtra, a caste Thorat would share with Ambedkar if both of
them had not rejected the caste system so completely. Ambedkar's
centrality to this upsurge needs no reiteration; and we would advance
the cause of understanding by pushing the chain of influences back

to one of Ambedkar's own intellectual forebears, Jotirao Phule (1827–90). Gail Omvedt has recently produced a masterly account of the movement whose origins can be identified with Phule and which, in turn, provided at least a part of the stimulus for Ambedkar too; and I propose to draw upon Omvedt's work to indicate the magnitude of this influence.[2]

Even though Phule's contemporary B. G. Tilak dominated the Maharashtrian and larger politics of his time, in some ways he represented a continuation with the *ancien régime* of the Peshwas. In challenging this Brahminical dominance and, instead, articulating a world-view built upon the premises of equality and rationality, Phule established a firm claim to being the most original and penetrating figure in Maharashtra's recent social and cultural history. Coming from the Mali caste of cultivators, Phule broadened his attack upon the economic and administrative dominance of moneylenders and Brahmins so as to hit at the ideological foundations of Brahminism and of the caste system generally, including the practice of untouchability. The general theme of equality found expression in a demand for mass education, in order to breach its prevailing control by Brahmins, and also in a strong emphasis on the liberation of women. Several of these concerns were reflected in the wedding ceremony he sponsored which was

innovative in two ways: in dispensing with the Brahman priestly intermediaries, and in including in the central passage a strong promise by the husband that he will protect his wife and allow her such rights as education.[3]

Much of the activity of the Satyashodhak Samaj, the society for seeking truth, which Phule and his friends founded, was organized from village bases, and this included the publication of several Marathi language journals; yet, what gave the movement its vitality on the ground served also to hide it from many of those who sought to function at a 'national' level.

It is clear from Omvedt's material that the Satyashodhak Samaj had acquired considerable influence in Vidarbha, the region of eastern Maharashtra where Thorat's village is located, by the early years of the twentieth century. Thorat tells me that he is unable to think of any influence that this movement might have had on the landowners and other high castes in his village, but he knows of several institutional complexes associated with this movement in the Vidarbha region. Thorat also considers reasonable the presumption that these institutions and the people and ideas associated with them could have been important reference points when, for example, the village landowners were faced with the social upsurge described by Thorat in his essay. (See also note 4.)

If so, the influence of Phule and the Satyashodhak Samaj on Thorat's life-space would be twofold. There is first the influence via Ambedkar: it can be seen in the determination of Thorat's family and of its neighbours to reshape their lives in a way that would command greater consideration from the larger society. In the process was forged the ideology which provided a coherent and supportive explanation for Thorat's observations and experiences; furthermore, in Milind College and elsewhere, Thorat was led into a range of social relationships and activities which, collectively, attacked the structure of ideas and relationships which had been the source of his youthful humiliation. Students coming to the college found there the crucial setting wherein they could support and reinforce changes in each other's frameworks of ideas concerning oneself and one's relations with the world.

The second source of Phule's influence acted, if indirectly, upon the village landowners, themselves of the middle castes, and long the victims of Brahmin and moneylender highhandedness. It is to this influence that, I think, we have to attribute the nature of their response to the Mahar show of independence in taking to Buddhism: after a boycott for a couple of months, they resumed the earlier pattern of economic relationship with the Mahars. The response was in terms not of a crushing show of power—such as landowners have often made in other regions—but of a willingness, howsoever grudgingly enacted, to accommodate the Mahar determination to forge new identities. This willingness, and the influence which probably induced it, also call for recognition.*

---

* In a comment on this passage, Mr Thorat attributes the restraint in the Maratha landowners' response to:

(1) *education*: especially the many colleges and schools affiliated to the Shivaji Education Society which was established by Punjabrao Deshmukh, which were essentially urban institutions that did much to transmit Phule's impulse for greater education to the landowning Marathas drawn from the villages.

(2) *politics*: the village leaders' involvement in the lower tiers of elective politics, from Gram Panchayat to Zila Parishad, increasing sharply in the mid-50s and exposing them (a) to a presumably more tolerant perspective among their urban caste-mates, active politically and often intellectually, and

2

Indicative of Mr Thorat's reflective bent of mind was a question he asked when his essay was in a late draft: how far can one generalize from a single case such as his? I suggest that his case belongs to a large class of situations. He has built upon the fortunate combination of a supportive ideology and initially the prospects of, and later the access to, reasonably satisfactory work opportunities: while on leave from his lectureship at Vasantrao Naik College, Aurangabad, he has virtually completed his M. Phil. thesis at Jawaharlal Nehru University and should soon enter the Ph.D. programme. This work situation appears to me to be important, for it gives one the secure base from which to mount an orderly attack upon the social targets of one's wrath.

This sort of combination has been available elsewhere too, often with comparable consequences: it applies to the North American blacks who emerge as successful professionals; to Africans—and other victims of colonialism—as they capture the reins of power; and as the earlier adversaries are softened or expelled, and the contours of one's social world change, the bitterness of earlier years is often dissolved in the dynamics of effort and achievement.

Mr Thorat's is a case concerning the transition out of a subordinate—indeed, stigmatized—group into a situation free from that sort of subordination by birth. The transition was made easier because, at a certain historical juncture, certain forces, which had long been gaining strength slowly, converged so as to reduce the weight of that particular sort of subordination. This has been attempted, however, as part of the establishment of a capitalist order. There is in this order an inbuilt accelerator to inequality, especially prior to the creation of (or with the dismantling of) a state-organized redistribu-

---

(b) to an appreciation of the electoral importance of the Harijan vote in elections in the village level.

(3) *the region's religious tradition*: apart from the social reformers like Ranade, Phule, Ambedkar, and Shinde, Maharashtra has also had a tradition of itinerant saints: one of them, Gadage Baba, came to Thorat's village three or four times, performed devotional *kirtan* before large audiences, and his discourses were very critical of the caste system and blind faith.

(4) *agrarian economy*: the increasing subdivision of inherited Maratha lands pushed some Marathas into the marginal and submarginal categories, sometimes forcing them to work as labourers alongside lower caste workers; this experience, too, served to make them more tolerant of their fellow labourers whose caste happened to be low.

tive neutralizer. When this order takes the capital-intensive road in a country with India's poverty levels, it breeds its own inexorable modes of subordination, of exclusion from opportunity, associated rationalizations, symbols, rituals, and humiliations.

This central thrust towards increasing secular inequality entails that, constitutional injunctions and political rhetoric notwithstanding, the resources transferred to the poorest groups can only be of a token sort, even though these might be substantial enough to make a difference to some individuals. Thorat's account is important not only because it documents one man's struggle against heavy odds and his capacity to transcend his own sense of humiliation but also because it indicates the fearsome odds that would confront, say, a Harijan landless labourer's daughter in the village. Thorat's father does own four acres of land, his two elder brothers are persuaded to suppress their own desire for education and to strengthen the family's income, and his brothers as well as his parents are utterly devoted to the cause of Thorat's education. By any reckoning these are exceptionally fortunate circumstances; to add to them, in his region, there are the legacies of Phule and Ambedkar, and the Ambedkar movement has been especially potent in stimulating Mahar aspirations for educational achievement, regardless of sacrifices it entailed. It takes this extraordinary combination to enable Thorat, via the Milind College, to set a relatively secure and acceptable course into the ranks of the intelligentsia. There is a distortive tendency, often unwittingly so, among social scientists and others to highlight success stories of this sort, implicitly exaggerating the chances of an untouchable child making this kind of transition. When Thorat asks, how far can one generalize from a single case such as his, the answer has to be: not very much so long as India's economic process is geared to the increasing of inequalities and so long as the political process serves to nurture and to stimulate, not to neutralize, the implications of that economic process.

3

Thorat's passionate assertions of the untouchable's preference for equality, fraternity, etc. evoke further pathos; for history's legacy, ambiguous as always, includes not only Phule and Ambedkar but also a social structure which makes Thorat himself somewhat vulnerable to critics of a certain sort. Put briefly, Thorat's critic can turn around—as indeed an eminent participant during the seminar did turn around—and ask, 'I am one with you in your demand for equality and fraternity; yet the social movement you discuss has been limited largely to the Mahars. The Mangs, the Chambhars, and other untouchable castes even in Maharashtra have not joined the movement, and the different castes stay substantially apart. What do you have to say on this persistence of virtual untouchability *within* the untouchable ranks?' The implication is clear: set your own house in order![4]

The question was raised by a distinguished sociologist, yet it betrays a certain innocence regarding modern India's social history. All levels of Indian society have long been heavily segmented; and, shorn of its taunt, the question above can be recast into the form: why has segmentation persisted among the untouchables when some upper caste enclaves, especially in the urban areas, have been undergoing desegmentation? The answer is written over the literature concerning the past two hundred years and turns upon (1) the differential access to educational opportunities, greatly favouring some strategically located urban groups, (2) the formation of new, overlapping economic interest groups in those enclaves in the colonial and the postcolonial milieu, and (3) the consequent flurry of movement for reform, questioning some of the old lines of segmentation in the strata affected.[5]

These processes have touched the lowest castes, at best, in a nominal measure, and therefore the corresponding pressures for erasing their segmental boundaries have been weak. On the other hand, their growing dependence upon the landowners, noted by Thorat early in his essay, has increased their sense of insecurity, pushing them all the more firmly into the familiar, if constricting, grooves of their own castes. Its implications for the capacity of the poor and the propertyless organizing themselves in support of their own interests are obvious.

The overall point is clear. Thorat's case provides India's dominant groups little reason to flaunt their much-vaunted liberalism. Seen against the backdrop of larger social and historical processes, it is rather more of an indictment.

NOTES AND REFERENCES

1. Erik H. Erikson, *Childhood and Society*, New York, W. W. Norton and Co., 1963, Chapter 1 and elsewhere.

2. Gail Omvedt, *Cultural Revolt in a Colonial Society: the Non-Brahman Movement in Western India, 1873 to 1930,* Bombay, Scientific Socialist Education Trust, 1976.

3. Ibid., pp. 111–12.

4. See also I. P. Desai, *Untouchability in Rural Gujarat,* Bombay, Popular Prakashan, 1976, Chapter 2.

5. The issues will be analysed at length in a work now in progress. For an interim statement, see my 'Urbanism in India: a socio-historical perspective', *Contributions to Indian Sociology,* 1977, n.s. 11, no. 1, in press.

7

REFLECTIONS ON THE SOCIAL CONSTRUCTION OF ADULTHOOD

VEENA DAS

1

An enquiry into the nature of adulthood in India has to necessarily begin with the concept of the person. Contrary to common sense notions in the West, the concept of the person as bounded, indivisible, and separate from his actions is not universally shared. In the conceptual systems of South Asia, the individual is seen as constantly being transformed by his transactions with others since he can convey the essence of his nature and receive the essence of others by entering into relationships of transaction.[1] As we shall see in the course of our exposition, the social roles and values associated with adulthood derive their meaning from these culturally shared notions about the person.

Anthropologists normally dissect social reality into separate spheres of kinship, economics, politics, religion, and others. They then treat each of these sub-systems as if they were bounded and had not only separate analytical statuses but also separate ontological statuses. The concepts of role and role-framework have been the traditional aids of the anthropologist for viewing reality in this manner. In this paper I shall attempt a different mode of analysis. Using the concept of the life-cycle[2] I shall try to show that the construction of everyday reality makes use of concepts which cut across the distinctions of religion, politics, economics, and kinship. In other words, I wish to examine whether the concept of person helps us to view adulthood within an integrated social reality. Let me hasten to add that by talking of an integrated social reality I do not mean to imply that there is a single definition of reality. Indeed, I am acutely aware that there are competing definitions of reality. The manner in which choices are made between these alternatives to define adulthood is one of the themes of this paper.

2

As the title of this paper indicates, it is reflective in nature. I have drawn the data presented here from different sources, but have made the most extensive use of data collected during my fieldwork among urban Punjabis in 1974–5, some of which have been reported earlier.[3] I have also drawn materials from popular fiction and from the sociological studies of other regions. In general, however, the description revolves around upper caste urban Punjabis. During my fieldwork I did not have the same kind of access to the world of men as I did to the world of women, which is why the emphasis of this paper is on the life-cycle of women.

It will be obvious to the most casual observer of Punjabi society that sons and daughters in a family are endowed with different significance. Many observers have noted the differences in the manner in which boys and girls are brought up in Hindu families, emphasizing the preferential treatment given to boys. One needs to be careful, however, in assuming that a single definition of reality is operative here.

It is true that sons are seen as future heirs, and parents look upon them for support in their old age. In contrast, girls are seen as belonging to a different family altogether and their socialization stresses their future roles as wives. However, daughters never cease to be the repositories of their family honour, and though parents cannot depend upon them for fulfilment of material needs, they do look upon them as symbols of the honour of their families. 'The prestige (*izzat*) of a family is in the hands of its daughters' is a common refrain which a girl may expect to hear many times a day from her parents.

The treatment of the body in childhood emphasizes separate value orientations for boys and girls. Hershman[4] has shown that while boys were often left naked in the Punjabi village he studied, great care was taken to see that the genitals of a baby-girl were properly covered. It was common for elder women to kiss or fondle a baby-boy's genitals and, in fact, separate linguistic terms exist in Punjabi for the genitals of a boy as distinct from the genitals of a male adult. The female genitals, however, are designated by a single term. Hershman feels that the terms for female genitals (*chuta*) is linked with the general terms for impurity (*chhuta*) and he tries to show that the source of all impurities is seen in the biological functions of women.

At the level of ritual, however, a reverse order also seems to be operative. A girl who has not menstruated is considered to be a *kanjak*, the embodiment of a goddess. There are several ritual occasions on which she is required to be ceremonially worshipped by her male kin. As the embodiment of goddess Lakshmi for her natal kin, she has a ritually privileged position. If her natal kin would allow her to touch their feet, it would lead to the incurring of sin for them.

The onset of puberty, metaphorically referred to as the 'appearance of pollen', is seen all over India as signalling the physiological maturity of the girl. In some parts of India a special ceremony is held to 'announce' the event to the near kin. The girl is henceforth treated as impure during menstruation and is subject to special taboos. The severity of the taboos varies from region to region. Till recently, in many parts of southern India, menstruating women had to move to an 'outhouse' specially reserved for them.

Among urban Punjabis the onset of menstruation is not 'announced' publicly by means of ritual. In fact, the Punjabi women treat menstruation as a private matter and try to ensure that the male members do not get an inkling of the state. They would be horrified by such public 'announcement' of menstruation either by means of ritual or by enforcement of taboos that are obvious to all.

Punjabi women do consider themselves impure during menstruation and are required to observe certain taboos, but in a discreet manner. For instance, a menstruating girl is required to refrain from touching preserves and pickles which, it is believed, would rot if she touched them. Though no part of the house is taboo for her, it is assumed that she will not offer worship during menstruation. Similarly, however young she is when she begins to menstruate, a girl should not sit on her father's or brother's lap when she is menstruating. What is of interest is that unlike the case of south India, a menstruating girl's state is never acknowledged or ritually announced to all members of the household. The taboos and the consequences of violating these are conveyed from senior female relatives to the younger ones and the girl is left to find her own excuses if faced with awkward circumstances.

Among Punjabi families that were studied, the implications of menstruation for the sexuality of women are considered far more serious than its implications for impurity. From this point onwards, a woman's sexuality is regarded as a great source of danger. As many writers have pointed out, the main threat to the purity of the caste comes from the sexuality of women. However, I think that in the Punjabi case the major emphasis would be on the honour of the family rather than the purity of the caste. Therefore, a young girl is constantly watched by her elder relatives. She is taught how to cover her breasts with her veil, to keep away from boys, and look towards the house as a major sphere of activity. This may completely confuse or bewilder the young girl who has not been taught to expect this, especially if she is the eldest female sibling. It has been my experience with informants in this age group that they strongly resent the new curbs on their freedom. But perhaps the best description of this process may be had from a novel by Krishna Sobti,[5] where the young heroine, Pasho, reminisces:

Those sweet days of childhood appeared before me. Sometimes granny would bathe me and dress me in new clothes and Mamu (MB) would say lovingly, 'She sits quietly like a doll as if she were the embodiment of an innocent goddess.' The first time when I came with my ears and nose pierced, I was wearing black thread in my ears and nose. Mamu said to granny, 'Mother, if you'd listen to me, buy her black stones for her ears and nose. On this milky white complexion, they'd be utterly beautiful.' Granny interrupted him, saying, 'Say something auspicious, son. For this beauty let there be diamonds and pearls.' My Mamu would pull my long tresses lovingly and I would giggle. Those days of love and affection passed so quickly. I became big. Neither was my childhood left, nor the openness of childhood. Every time I came across Mamu now, I was taunted. After bathing in the well, I'd get the barber's wife to comb my hair and I'd rejoice in my clean clothes. But Mamu would give me looks of sarcasm. Granny would remind me again and again, 'Cover yourself properly, girl.' If I looked happy, they'd say, 'Don't sit dreaming, do some work.'

I'd listen and listen. Neither could I understand anything; nor could I say anything.

This case was perhaps a little extreme since Pasho's mother had eloped with a Muslim and left Pasho to be brought up in her mother's house, and all the fears of her uncles for the honour of their family had become crystallized round her person. Nevertheless, approximations to these sentiments were often obtained in my conversations with my informants of this age group.

At this stage an explicit or implicit contrast between the 'woman of the home' and a 'wanton woman' also begins to be made. The girl is often called *kullachini*, one with bad omens, if she fails to cover herself or tries to adorn herself or for any number of offences. As will be shown later, the contrast between 'woman of the home' and a harlot is explicitly made in judging the behaviour of women in adolescence and young adulthood. It is perhaps not accidental that a play on the same symbols can express the notion of a 'woman of the home' and a wanton woman. The veil when used properly to cover is the symbol of a daughter or a wife. When it is pulled away, carelessly draped, or accidentally dropped, it may be seen as an invitation to an illicit love affair. Many songs of *mujra*, the recitals given by singing girls or prostitutes, play on the theme of the lover pulling away the veil of the harlot. Similarly, the nose-ring which is a very important symbol of a bride can be used in a dual manner. The virgin girl who becomes a bride *wears* her nose-ring, perhaps symbolizing the binding of her sexuality to one man. The highest bidder for a virgin being introduced to prostitution, however, gets the right to *remove* her nose-ring. One last example from the famous ballad of 'Heer Ranjha' may suffice. When Heer's love affair with Ranjha is discovered, her mother reprimands her, saying, 'When a daughter obeys the norms of decency she is an honour to her family. When she becomes wanton, she is a prostitute. Heer, we thought we had a rose in our garden but alas it turned out to be a thorn.'

If a girl follows the norms of modesty, she is considered to be precious to her parents. Parents treat their daughters not only as the future wives of another family in whose hands their honour rests, but also as privileged guests. As one informant said, 'Daughters are comparable to something kept in trust for another (*amanat*). You have to care for them, love them, and you will be held responsible for them but you are destined to lose them. Indeed, once a daughter is properly married and goes to her own house, it is like a debt that has been paid.'

The most poignant moment in a wedding is when the parents take leave of the daughter saying, 'We have cared for you to the best of our ability. If, inadvertently, we have done something to offend you please forgive us.' The daughter, while departing, throws some wheat over her shoulder towards her natal house, symbolizing that though she is leaving, she is not taking away all the prosperity with her.

With marriage, a girl moves over to the house of her husband. In the initial few years of marriage, a girl is constantly shifting between her parents' house and her husband's house. Not only the Punjabis, but also Hindus belonging to other regions, have proverbs to express the open familiarity which a girl enjoys in her father's house and the constraints of her husband's house. Carstairs[6] recorded the proverb from Deoli, 'Ghar mein lado, bahar chori', a free translation of which would be 'A little loved one in her parent's house and a respectable woman in her husband's house.'

The symbol which expresses the constraints of a newly married girl best is the veil. In her husband's house a girl has to cover herself from all her elder male affinal relatives. The most appropriate norms for her are the norms of social invisibility. Descriptions in fictional literature suggest that the contrast between a 'woman of the house' and a wanton woman does not cease even in the privacy of the bedroom. When Mitro, a heroine of Krishna Sobti's novel *Mitro Marjani*,[7] tries to seduce her husband, he says 'Why are you dressed like a harlot (*kanjari*)?'

The marriage ritual of Hindus emphasizes the 'oneness' of the husband and the wife. Terms for the wife like *sahadharmini* and *ardhangini* point to the wife as an equal partner of the husband. However, the wife is not only a stranger in the husband's house, she also stands for the potential breakdown of the joint family. Thus while the norms stress the complete incorporation of the wife in the husband's group, women appear in fact as Janus-faced creatures belonging to the husband's group and yet being strangers to it. Let me give two examples of the dual position of women in the husband's house.

The first example is from a story recorded by Temple in *The Legends of the Punjab*,[8] the story of King Rasalu. When King Rasalu was born, astrologers predicted that if his father were to glimpse him even once before he was twelve, he (the father) would die. So King Rasalu was kept in a secluded castle till he was almost twelve. He managed to escape and during his voyage over many lands he came across many pretty girls. But whenever a proposal of marriage was made, he had a standard answer: 'The pasture is strange and this is a foreign land. You are a stranger's daughter (*begani dhi*). If I, a stranger, get ensnared, who will save me?' His fear of the stranger's daughter was so intense that he finally married an infant girl, took her away from her parents' house to be brought up under his own care so that when Koklan, the bride, reached puberty she did not even know whether Rasalu was her brother or husband. The poignancy of the story lies in the fact that even Koklan, brought up so strictly by her own husband and guarded with such care, betrays him to the first stranger who seduces her.

My second example is from my own field notes, about a man who had died in Lahore in 1922 at the age of twenty-four, two years after his marriage. His brother, who is now nearing sixty, alleged that he was poisoned by his wife so that she may appropriate his money and the jewellery which had been given to her. When I remarked that it was a little difficult to think of his own wife poisoning him, the immediate answer was that she was, after all, a stranger. I have described elsewhere[9] the manner in which a girl's natal family is always ready to protect her against her conjugal kin. The death of a bride in the early years of her marriage is often the subject of acrimonious debate with accusations of neglect and cruelty being hurled on her conjugal kin and denials coming with equal vehemence from them. I noted in a paper elsewhere that the State Government of Punjab was recently led to pass an ordinance stipulating that every death of a woman in her husband's house in the first seven years of her marriage has to be investigated as a criminal case. So great is the suspicion between a woman's natal kin and her conjugal kin in the first few years of marriage.

Marriage legitimizes sex but the attitudes to sexuality are riddled with contradictions. Once a woman's body has been made the subject of a man's sexual desires she becomes forever contaminated. My informants would often say: 'A woman's body is contaminated (made *juṭhī*) every day.' I have translated the term *juṭhī* by contaminated here, but I would also like to stress that *juṭhī* implies that it is consumed every day. The woman's body is then not only a source of contamination for men but also for her own self. Mitro, the heroine of Krishna Sobti's novel *Mitro Marjani*, is told by her sister-in-law:[10]

Don't be proud of your body. There are thousands of women like you who have two eyes, two hands, a nose, a mouth, and yes, even breasts like yours. There is nothing to be proud of in a woman's body. It is contaminated (becomes *juṭhī*) every day. Think of God, think of the hereafter if you want to purify it.

One more example from Temple's[11] *The Legends of the Punjab* may suffice in pointing out the widespread notion of the woman being contaminated by sex, rather like left-over food. In this, the story of Shila Devi, the king tries to seduce his minister's wife who rebuffs him by saying,

> *Tu hai merā rājrā, tu hai merā māna*
> *Main teri huṃ Brahmani, tu mere jajman*
> *Voh ki rājā salāhiye, jo juṭh begāni khān.*

You are my king, you are my respected one.
I am your Brahmani, you are my jajman.
How shall I praise a king who is ready
To take another man's leavings (*juṭh*).

It is significant that a man's body is not made impure (*juṭhā*) by
sexual intercourse since it is the woman who is seen as the vessel. For
a man, sexuality includes the power to procreate. People assume that
if a man is sterile, he would also be impotent or sexually inadequate.
In cases of childlessness, it is very important for a family's honour
to be able to lay the blame on the woman. If a woman is childless
(*bānjha*), she is considered inauspicious or unfortunate but it does not
bring her natal family's honour into question. On the other hand,
sterility and sexual inadequacy in a man is a charge which could put
to question the honour of his entire family. I was told that in earlier
times a charge of impotence levelled against a man by his wife or her
family could lead to lasting feuds and murders among the two
families.

Despite the notions about sexuality described above, it is also
said to create strong bonds between a man and a woman. Though
the moral norms do not allow any public display of intimacy between
husband and wife, it is recognized that sexuality may create strong
bonds that might negate the earlier bonds of a man with his parents
or siblings. People often said that it is the nature of salt to melt in
water, or that magnet attracts iron, to explain a man's attraction to
his wife.

Just as a husband and wife are not expected to give any indication
of their close relationship in the presence of other members of the
family, so are parents expected to avoid cuddling their children in
public. So while both sexuality and procreation are taken to be
biologically necessary in young adulthood, the display of any
emotions based on these ties is not considered to be proper. It is
for this reason, it seems to me, that in this phase of her life-cycle
a woman feels most distant from the roles that she is expected to
play.

Goffman[12] formulated the concept of 'role distance' to describe
such a situation. He also advocated that a difference be made between
the concepts of 'primary adjustment' and 'secondary adjustment'. In
the context of organizations he emphasized that this referred to
unauthorized means employed by members to obtain unauthorized
ends. As he pointed out, secondary adjustments arise not only in

formal institutions, but also in the case of the individual's bondage to other types of social institutions or roles.

The moral prescriptions governing the phase of young adulthood in the life of a woman emphasize her 'social invisibility' in her husband's house. It is at this phase that many women employ numerous 'secondary adjustments' to their roles. For instance, they often manage to convey their 'distance' to their roles by the manner in which they fulfil all their obligations. I have elsewhere described[13] how a couple may fulfil all their obligations and yet convey the 'unreality' of this situation. I described the case of a man who beat up his wife when she quarrelled with his sister, thus maintaining the myth that he treated his wife as a stranger. Yet, the same night he successfully conveyed the information that the beating had been merely a performance, by making love to his wife in an indiscreet manner, showing that there had not been any real estrangement between them.

The point that I wish to stress is that identity may be defined by a person either through identification with roles, or a distinction may be made between role and self, portraying the roles as masks. It is in the phase of young adulthood that women experience the maximum role distance and identify their roles as masks which hide their true identities.

In the last phase of her adulthood, a woman may either be a wife or a widow. She is considered to have reached the last phase with the marriage of her eldest child (or menopause whichever is earlier). In this phase she is expected to relinquish all sexual relations with her husband even if he is alive. Many women often complained about the sexual demands of their husbands 'beyond all norms of decency'. Behaviour at this phase is strongly influenced by norms of asceticism, non-involvement and freedom from passions.

Widowhood is said to be the worst calamity that a woman may face. As Madan[14] has said, the death of a child may be seen as a personal calamity but the death of a husband is seen as altering the social identity of a woman. The Punjabi word for widow, *raṇḍi*, which is never used in polite discourse, is significantly also the word for a prostitute. One of the legends recorded by Temple[15] seems to suggest that this linguistic identity is not accidental. In the story of Shila Devi quoted earlier, the king does not succeed in seducing his minister's wife, Shila. Nevertheless, when the minister returns from his voyage, he finds a ring which the king had left behind in Shila's bedroom. Enraged, he accuses Shila of infidelity and orders the maids to take away all signs of wifehood from her and to *dress her as a widow*. When word reaches Shila's parents that she is forced to dress as a widow and eat only one meal a day, they immediately conclude that she has been accused of infidelity. It seems likely to me that in the case when a man dies in his youth, his wife may be held somehow responsible for his death by not being entirely true to him. This was not often expressed explicitly, and since I had not given enough thought to the linguistic identity between prostitute and widow, I failed to look into this matter.

The Punjabis maintained a distinction between a girl who was widowed before her instinctual urges had been satisfied and a woman who was widowed in her old age. People reiterated the view that if one died before the instinctual urges of sexuality and generativity had been satisfied, then one would become a ghost. Sometimes they would even attribute feelings of jealousy to a goddess who had remained unmarried, saying that she was inflicting misfortunes due to jealousy.

The norms of widowhood are essentially norms of asceticism. The basic emphasis is on white clothes, simple *satvik* food, i.e. pure food which does not produce passions. As I shall argue later, it seems to me that the norms of asceticism provide a transcendence of the morality of particularistic groups and positions. Widows, being on the margins of society, represent a balance which the system achieves through transcendence. But they share this, to an extent, with all old people as we shall see in the next section.

If a woman was very old, a difference between the statuses of wife and widow was not noticeable. It was remarkable that people felt no embarrassment in discussing death and their reactions to it. Most women were emphatic that they did not wish to die away from home. The observance of proper death rituals was seen as necessary and important, both by the young and the old. A strong emphasis was placed at this stage on reconciling differences and being ready to face death with equanimity. As one old woman said of death, 'It is like being shifted from one breast to the other breast of the mother. The child feels lost in that one instant, but not for long.'[16] The Hindu rituals to ancestors assume that though death terminates a social relationship, it continues within a cosmic framework. The reiteration of a cycle, that death was like another birth, occurred in discussion with most informants as also the view that in face of death the identities they had assumed merge into some wider cosmic identity.

3

In the course of my fieldwork, I did not have the same kind of access to the world of men as I did to the world of women. Nevertheless, some striking points of contrast or similarity may be discussed here.

In the case of a woman, the physiological changes are accompanied by shifts from one phase to another. Menstruation, assumption of adult sexuality, childbirth, and menopause are all accompanied by important changes in the social status. Such shifts in status are not easily visible in the case of men, since these are not always ritualized. One or two points of interest may be noted here.

As mentioned earlier, the marriage of a man brings to the fore the conflict between his ties with his mother and the ties with his wife. In the marriage rituals of many regions, the continuing ties with the mother are symbolized for the bridegroom but not for the bride. Among the Coorgs, the bridegroom has to be fed milk by the mother from a round vessel with a spout (suggestive of the breast?) before he leaves for the bride's house. The protective qualities of the mother's milk are emphasized in other rituals. For instance, he has to be shaved on this occasion with milk and not water. His nail-pairings and shavings have to be placed in a plate of milk and then buried under a milk-exuding tree. If we remember that hair, nail-pairings, and shavings are potent elements with which a person may be harmed through magic or sorcery, the symbolism of milk seems to point to the protective power of the mother not only in childhood but throughout life. It is significant that this spout used in the marriage ritual is only broken at a person's death.

In contrast to the protective powers of his mother, the sexuality of his wife is represented as necessary but dangerous for a man. It is well known that sexual intercourse is considered dangerous for a man as it leads to loss of semen. Semen is considered to be concentrated blood and a woman who makes repeated demands on her husband can make him ill and tired; so that his semen becomes curdled and foul-smelling. In this context, it may also be pointed out that in-coming wives are regarded as powerful agents of the supernatural. They are bestowed with special powers and suspicions about *tona* or *jadu* are, by no means, rare. Thus the man in his young adulthood faces a peculiar contradiction whereby abstaining from sex is considered to bestow great power and good health and yet satisfaction of instinctual urges is also considered necessary. As we shall see, this contradiction between asceticism and eroticism appears in many forms in Hindu thought and mythology, and one of the manifestations of this contradiction can be seen in the norms of sexuality for the householder.

If adulthood involves adult, procreative sexuality, it also involves the access to property and other productive resources of the community. In many societies, however, a distinction is made between a man whose father is alive and one whose father is dead. As Fortes remarked for the Tallensi, a nine-year-old whose father is dead may be treated as a jural adult and a forty-year-old man whose father is alive may be treated like a jural child. It was rare among the Punjabis to partition the household as long as the father was alive. This meant that sons continued to be under the jural authority of their fathers, normally handing them their earnings, and following the decisions made by the father. Similarly, in inter-personal relations it was considered a breach of moral norms for a man to take an aggressive stand in the affairs of the *birdari* or the local community, except to support the father. Carstairs[17] noted that the only men in Deoli who dared to cuddle their children were those whose fathers were dead. Thus the articulation between physiological maturity and jural adulthood seems much looser for men than for women. But as I said earlier, having limited access to the world of men, I cannot compare the objective roles and subjective identities of adulthood for men.

Before I move on to the concluding section, I would like to comment on the increasing decline of sex role differentiation in old age. Whereas women in the early phases of adulthood are expected to cover their bodies, there is a relative lack of concern about the body in old age. In fact, one may find old women with uncovered breasts or the flimsiest of saris without their provoking any comment. At this age they also acquire a privileged position to ask awkward questions or remind younger people of their moral obligations. For instance, a very old woman may question the bride about the sexual potency of her husband, though this topic could be approached only with the greatest of difficulties by any other relatives. Similarly, old men may comment on the behaviour of younger people in a manner of privileged familiarity. To give an instance, there was considerable gossip about a girl who had given birth to a baby seven months after her marriage though her parents had told everyone that she had given birth to a premature baby. A man of seventy, when asked if he had congratulated the mother, said he would do so only after nine months. This comment was repeated to the girl's parents but they ignored it saying that it was the comment of a senile man. A similar comment by a younger person, more involved in the affairs of the *birdari*, could have led to a serious fight. It is felt that in old age people become free of the particular roles to which they were bound in the early phases of their lives. The burdens of their roles are lifted and they are offered a kind of 'release'.

The Theory of Ashramas

It will have been noted that I have discussed the different phases in the life-cycle without reference to the theory of *ashramas*, on which both Erikson[18] and Kakar[19] lay some emphasis for the understanding of adulthood and identity in India. I do not believe that this difference of approach can be traced to the different types of sources that we have used. Rather, it seems to me that the theory of *ashramas* is one attempt at reconciling the opposite ends of *samsara* and *moksha*, eroticism and asceticism, and like all myths it only succeeds in giving an apparent resolution to the fundamental contradictions of Hindu society.

The theory of *ashramas* is seen by Erikson and Kakar as dividing the life-span into four distinct stages. Yet the artificiality of the scheme is obvious as it combines stages which are optional with stages which are obligatory. As Dumont[20] has reminded us, we should be careful in distinguishing a genuine whole from one in which elements have been added to make up a sacred number.

Dumont's analysis suggests that the theory of *ashramas* centres round a contrast between the man-in-the-world and the renouncer. The former is located in the world of caste and householdership while the latter represents an asocial state apart from society proper. In this context I would like to suggest that the man-in-the-world represents the normative system of bounded, structured, particularistic groups corresponding to the closed morality of Henri Bergson. In contrast, the outsider, the *sanyasi*, stands for a wider morality of humanity, transcending the close morality of particularistic bounded groups. It is in this sense that the *sanyasi* can be seen as representing the whole society at one and the same time, whereas those who are within the society can represent only parts of it. The 'balance' in the system is provided by the concept of transcendence.

This transcendence of the bounded morality of particularistic groups may also be affected by the active eroticism of the Tantric traditions. The same elements by being placed into a different system may get totally different meanings. For instance, sexual love plays a different role in the morality of the householder and the morality of the Tantric. As Wendy O'Flaherty says, 'In the *tantric* tradition, *svakīyā* love leads to procreation and is useless for religious release. On the other hand, *parakīyā* (adulterous) love leads to non-involvement and religious release. *Svakīyā* love leads to immortality through procreation while *parakīyā* love leads to immortality through release.'[21]

This conflict between asceticism and eroticism, as different ways of relating to the sacred and as ways of defining one's identity, recurs as a constant theme in Hindu mythology. The conflicts of the ascetic Shiva and the erotic Shiva are well known in mythology. At a different level the emphasis on sexual withdrawal as a source of strength and indulgence as a source of gratification, the conflicts between *tapa* (austerity) and *kama* (desire) manifest themselves in different ways in defining the ordinary man's attitude to sex. The theory of *ashramas* seeks to resolve this conflict by assigning a controlled eroticism to the stage of the householder and affirming that asceticism is reserved only for the last stage of one's life when one's instinctual urges have been satisfied. This, however, is only an apparent resolution and the wider morality of the man who represents the sentiment of humanity forms a consistent threat to the morality of the man who is located in the particularistic structures of caste and householdership. Two examples from eminent works of literature make the same point far more eloquently.

The first example is from Premchand's *Godan*.[22] Matadin, the son of the proud Brahmin, has been living with an untouchable woman, Celia. True to rules of caste morality, he is careful never to accept food from his mistress. The Chamars are enraged and they force some meat in Matadin's mouth publicly. But the morality of the Brahmin finds an answer to this also. Matadin has to undergo expiation and after he has given a dinner to the elders of his caste, he is purified and is accepted back into the caste fold. However, he has to break all relations with Celia. After some time Matadin repents in the real sense of the term. This time he decides to break all relations with the Brahmins and to marry Celia. In explaining his conduct he says 'I have violated the rules of the caste-exclusiveness. But beyond the morality of caste, there is the morality of humanity. The village may find me guilty, but god will not.' Here he finds true maturity in the transcendence of his bounded, closed morality.

The second example is from *Samskara* by Anantha Murthy.[23] Commenting on the allegorical character of the novel, Ramanujan says:

Praneshacharya often wonders whether there is not a serious side to Naranappa's mockery and sensuality; whether sacrilege is not a 'left-handed' way of attaining the sacred. By an ancient inversion, salvation is as possible through intoxication as by self-discipline, through violation as through observance of the Law. The Lord may even be reached sooner through hate than by devotion. Naranappa's way gathers strength by enlisting, and not defying instinctual urges. Praneshacharya himself remembers out of his past in Banaras, another Naranappa-like figure, fellow-pupil Mahabala. Mahabala gave up the 'strait and narrow' of Sanskritic learning and found 'reality' in a whore in the holy city itself.

NOTES AND REFERENCES

1. This argument derives from the writings of Mckim Marriott, Ronald Inden and Ralph Nicholas. In this context, see Mckim Marriott and Ronald Inden, 'Caste Systems', in *Encyclopedia Britannica*, 15th Edition, Chicago, 1974.
2. The use of the concept of the life-cycle derives more from anthropology than from psychology here. It seems to me that cross-cultural comparisons are necessary to see whether the stages of the life-cycle can be constructed without regard to the specificities of a given culture.
3. See my 'Masks and Faces: An Essay on Punjabi Kinship', in *Contributions to Indian Sociology*, New Series, vol. 10, no. 1, 1976.
4. Paul Hershman, 'Pure and Impure', mimeo., 'Hair, Sex, and Dirt in Punjabi Culture', *Man*, Journal of the Royal Anthropological Institute, 1964.
5. Krishna Sobti, *Dāra se Bichḍī*, Hind Pocket Books, 1961.
6. Morris G. Carstairs, *The Twice Born: A Study of a Community of High Caste Hindus*, London, The Hogarth Press, 1968.
7. Krishna Sobti, *Mitro Marjānī*, Hind Pocket Books, 1963.
8. R. C. Temple, *The Legends of the Punjab*, Education Society Press, Bombay, 1884.
9. See my 'Masks and Faces: An Essay on Punjabi Kinship'.
10. See note 7.
11. See note 8.
12. Erving Goffman, *Asylums*, Penguin Books, 1968.
13. See note 9.
14. T. N. Madan, 'The Structural Implications of Marriage among Kashmiri Brahmins', *Contributions to Indian Sociology*, NS, vol. 9, 1975.
15. See note 8.

16. This analogy is found in Rabindranath Tagore's *Gitanjali*. This woman could hardly read Hindi and had certainly not read the works of Tagore. It seems likely to me that she had heard this analogy in a public lecture in the Arya Samaj which she attended every week and it had made a very deep impression on her. It is also possible that this was a folk notion which reached the poet and was given a poetic transformation by him.

17. See note 6.

18. Erik H. Erikson, 'The Life Cycle', in *International Encyclopaedia of Social Sciences*, New York, Macmillan and the Free Press, 1969.

19. See his contribution in this volume.

20. See Louis Dumont, 'World Renunciation in Indian Religions', in *Religion, Politics, and History in India*, Houton, 1970.

21. Wendy O'Flaherty, *Eroticism and Asceticism in the Mythology of Shiva*, London, Oxford University Press, 1973.

22. Munshi Premchand, *Godan*, Allahabad, Saraswati Press, 1936.

23. U. R. Anantha Murthy, *Samskara: A Rite For a Dead Man*, Delhi, Oxford University Press, 1968, tr. by A. K. Ramanujan, p. 144.

8

SEARCH FOR AN IDENTITY

A Viewpoint of a Kannada Writer

U. R. ANANTHA MURTHY

'Some days past I have found a curious confirmation of the fact that
what is truly native can and often does dispense with local color; I
found this confirmation in Gibbon's *Decline and Fall of the Roman
Empire*. Gibbon observes that in the Arabian book *par excellence*, in
the Koran, there are no camels: I believe if there were any doubt as to
the authenticity of the Koran, this absence of camels would be sufficient
to prove it is an Arabian work. It was written by Mohammed, and
Mohammed, as an Arab, had no reason to know that camels were especially Arabian; for him they were a part of reality, he had no reason to
emphasize them; on the other hand, the first thing a falsifier, a tourist,
an Arab nationalist would do is have a surfeit of camels, caravans of
camels, on every page; but Mohammed, as an Arab, was unconcerned;
he knew he could be an Arab without camels.'

Jorge Luis Borges, 'The Argentine Writer and Tradition',
Labyrinths, New Directions, 1962, p. 181.

1

The situation could have turned into a series of laudatory speeches in
these days of seminars in India to celebrate centenaries of well-known
Indian and international figures. But the secretary of the Ministry of
Education which hosted the seminar to celebrate the Aurobindo
centenary was a sensitive Hindi poet, who made the occasion an
excuse to discuss problems of contemporary writing in the Indian
languages. After the Minister had paid the expected tributes to
Aurobindo and called upon the writers to uphold Indian culture,
work for national integration, world peace, etc., we settled down to
business. We had met in one of the dingy provincial capitals of north

This paper appeared earlier in *Writing From the World*, International Writing
Program, University of Iowa.

India, and among us we had writers in Hindi, Bengali, Marathi, and Kannada, and an internationally famous Indian painter.

The discussion inevitably turned to a topic that obsesses Indian writers these days: why is the western mode of thought and writing the model for us? Why aren't we original in our treatment of form and content in novel, drama, or poetry?

While Indian dance and music are uniquely Indian, why does contemporary Indian literature take its bearings from the literature of the West? Are we really a nation of mimics, victims of English education which has conditioned the faculties of our perception so much that we fail to respond freshly to the immediate situation in India? Should we read Brecht in order to discover that our folk theatre can be used? Why do we import even our radicalism via Ginsberg, Osborne, or Sartre? And our reaction against the West— isn't it often emotional, while intellectually we remain bound to western modes of thought?

But the language that we used to discuss these questions was English, as it had to be. And the names and examples that dominated our discussion were different from those fashionable ten years ago. In the place of Eliot and Yeats, dear to us for the impact of Indian philosophy on them, we used now the ideas of Camus, Kafka, Sartre, and Lukac's. We admired the achievement of Russian masters, who seemed better influences for us than the Anglo-Saxon writers who are antimetaphysical and pragmatic in their outlook. Wasn't the Russian literary scene before the revolution very similar to ours, in its struggle between the Westernizers and the Slavophiles? Dostoevsky with his metaphysical brooding was closer to the Indian temperament than the writers of the novels of manners. Still it was Shaw and Galsworthy, rather than the more poetic Synge and Chekhov, who influenced the previous generation of writers in India.

As we were discussing these questions, ironically with examples from the West rather than from our own literatures, some of which have a history of a thousand years, and quite a few writers radical and disturbing in their vision, the painter narrated to us an incident which deeply moved me. Before I relate what he said, let me describe how we dressed, which is important for the point I want to make.

The Bengali writer and a Hindi writer wore white dhotis and collarless long Indian shirts, which nearly all nationalist Indians wore during our struggle for freedom. The Bengali writer had a Marxist background (only he spoke in Bengali which was translated to us), and the Hindi writer was a Gandhian socialist of the Lohia school. Two Hindi writers and a Marathi writer, who were in their thirties and modernists in their writing, wore pants and jubba and had long hair—now the accepted attire of bohemian and artistic Indian intellectuals. (Even in this dress one looks middle class in India. The film stars have popularized it among the young of the rich and middle classes.) Only the painter looked authentically unmiddle class—with his flowing hair and beard, collarless shirt and dhoti not elegantly gathered and worn in the Bengali fashion, but tucked around the waist carelessly in the South Indian style. He could have been genuinely taken for a wandering Indian Sadhu except for his powerful and well articulated English. Perhaps a remark made by me in the course of the discussion on the search for Indian identity had prompted him to speak, or perhaps I am mistaken. Anyhow, this is what I had said.

Speaking of Kannada literature, I had observed that there were distinctly two generations of writers—those who belonged to the Gandhian era, and us. In order to clarify certain issues, I had ventured to generalize recklessly (which most of us were doing anyhow) and described these generations as 'insiders' and 'outsiders' respectively. Some 'insiders' even grew a tuft, wore caste marks, chewed betel, and, more often than not, came from a rural background. Along with their Gandhian idealism, their sensibilities bore the distinctive features of their castes and regions, and they wrote as if the English education they received was inconsequential. I had in my mind some great Kannada writers like Bendre, Putina, and Masti and I was of course rashly generalizing, for it was not unusual in the past to describe these writers as the Wordsworth, Shelley, Hardy, Shaw, etc., of Kannada. Yet I was not wholly wrong in thinking of them as 'insiders' in comparison with my generation of writers. There is no doubt we look and think differently from them. We admire their insider's knowledge of Indian tradition but reject their celebratory attitude toward Indian traditionalism. They made it possible for us to write, but we had to rebel against their conservative clinging to certain aesthetic modes. Some modern writers are, as a result, more inventive in their writing, but haven't we also moved closer to the West in our experimentation, thus risking rootlessness in our own tradition? I raised the question, but as a practising modernist writer myself I also tried to argue that there was no need to be unnecessarily anxious about it. We all write in the Indian languages, and this fact has a profound consequence on what we actually do in our languages, however much we expose ourselves to the West in search of ideas and forms. The 'insiders' and 'outsiders' can't remain mutually exclusive. The fact that we write in an Indian language like Kannada, kept alive by the oral traditions of the illiterate rural people, as well as a thousand-year-long native literary tradition, which has behind it an even longer pan-Indian Sanskrit tradition, has its own compulsion on what its recent writers do with their exposure to the West. Moreover, it can be said that many of our regional languages, despite their rich literary traditions, were actually preserved by illiteracy; for the literate of our country have always acquired the language of the ruling élites, whether it was Sanskrit, Persian, or English and tended to use the mother tongue as a dialect and the acquired language as the medium of intellectual discourse. The medium shapes the writer, even when he is shaping it. The writer influenced by the West may think and feel like an outsider, and yet he has to be an insider to the language created by the peculiar congruence of indigenous and Sanskrit classical traditions, folk tradition, and now the impact of spreading western education. If you borrow western technology and science, its culture too is bound to influence you, and where else can the integration of conflicting strains in our life be achieved except in one's language?

I was at pains not to appear eclectic in my approach. I wanted my friends to see the emergence of a new Indian identity in our literature as the result of a dialectic, not a mixture, of the living old and new, which would be germane to the genius of our languages. Kannada writers had such a relationship with Sanskrit literature once, and our achievement in the past was not a copy of Sanskrit but in some writers at least it was unique—although within the context of Sanskritic tradition. In my argument I had assumed that language rejects what is wilfully and artificially imported into it, and discerning literary criticism can distinguish between what is genuine and what is fake without going into the abstract and unsolvable question of how much of western influence is good for us.

Moreover, I argued, the language, Kannada, may have a literary tradition of a thousand years; still the contemporary writer can only use the current language that has become a part of his experience in his own lifetime. The search for the language adequate to one's creation is also a continuous one; it varies from one work to another.

When the writer influenced by western literatures chooses to write in a language like Kannada, he has made a moral choice. If the ideas that are still not of my language are embodied in my language creatively, then they become a part of the living tradition of my language.

I said that one uses only the current language of one's lifetime; but perhaps it is even narrower than this. As a writer I have felt often that my essential language is what I acquired during my childhood in a village and what I have been able to add to it—not superficially but experientially—in the process of growing up. In the actual business of writing don't we all know how much of our knowledge and our acquired language is really superfluous and useless? The magic of literary creation lies in actualizing new facets of experience; suggesting the inarticulate while articulating the particular and the given; conquering new domains of experience which are not yet the property of my language. If I should do all these in a language that has become my own only from the days of my childhood, then that language which has roots in me must have roots outside me as well—in its tradition of a thousand years, and what is affecting the lives of the people who speak that language today. If the western impact on us is a reality, how can we wish it away? I will have to relate myself to it with my language, which, if it has to have evocative power, should have its roots in the language of the ancient poets, and its current life in the idiomatic vigour of the illiterate peasant's speech.

As a creative writer I work on this assumption, but I can't wholly silence my literary conscience with that argument. Hence what the painter said, his extraordinary appearance and ability as an artist adding to the power of his argument, deeply disturbed me. In retrospect what he said may seem simple to me now, but the fact that I was disturbed by his argument (and a few other writers were also impressed like me), is an indication of a profound disquiet among the Indian writers today in their search for identity.

The painter was travelling through villages in north India studying folk-art. A lonely cottage at the foot of a hill attracted his eye. As he approached the cottage, he was puzzled by a piece of stone which he saw inside the cottage through the window; it was decorated with kunkum—the red powder that our women wear on their foreheads as an auspicious sign—and flowers. He wanted to photograph the stone the peasant worshipped and he asked the peasant who was weaving a basket outside the cottage if he could bring the stone outside the cottage into the sun so that he could take a picture. After taking the photograph, the painter apologized to the peasant in case the stone he worshipped was polluted by moving it outside. He had not expected the peasant's reply. 'It doesn't matter,' the peasant said, 'I will have to bring another stone and anoint kunkum on it.' Any piece of stone on which he put kunkum became God for the peasant. What mattered was his faith, not the stone. Do we understand the manner in which the peasant's mind worked?—the painter asked us. Can we understand his essentially mythical and metaphorical imagination which directed his inner life? Will Lukac's and Russell, who influence the structure of our thinking now, help us see instinctively the way this peasant's mind worked? That is why we don't understand the complex pattern of ancient Indian thought, its daring subjectivity, caught as we are in the narrow confines of western scientific rationality. In his simplicity the peasant still keeps alive the mode of thinking and perception, which at the dawn of human civilization revealed to the sages of the *Upanishads* the vision that Atman is Brahman. Shouldn't we prefer the so-called superstition of the peasant which helps him see organic connections between the animal world, human world and nature surrounding him, to the scientific rationality of western science that has driven the world into a mess of pollution and ecological imbalance?

The painter continued: western education has alienated us utterly from this peasant, who belongs to the category of the seventy per cent illiterate Indian mass. There is no gap for him between what he perceived subjectively and objectively. As his senses were actively engaged with the world outside him, he had no time to reflect on the luxury of the existentialist problem of whether life was meaningful. If we don't understand the structure and mode of this peasant's thinking, we can't become true Indian writers. Therefore we should free ourselves from the enslaving rationalist modes of western scientific thinking, from which even their great writers are not totally liberated. Only then we will be able to see what connects this peasant vitally to his world that surrounds him and to his ancestor, who perhaps ploughed the same patch of land some three thousand years ago. The western modes of perception will not help us understand what sustains this peasant—whether it is liberalism, scientific positivism, or even Marxism—these European-born theories only serve to make us feel inferior and thus turn our country into an imitation of the West.

As I said, we were moved by the painter's argument. In the midst of Camus, Sartre, Kafka, and Lukac's, he had stood before us an authentic Indian who was untouched by the ideas of any of these writers whom we were using as points of reference to define our positions.

In retrospect a doubt nagged me. Isn't the authentic Indian peasant, whose imagination is mythical and who relates to nature organically, also an imported cult figure of the western radicals who are reacting against their materialist civilization? What if these spiritual reactions in the West are their way of keeping fit, and the 'decline of the West' theory is glibly repeated humbug?

In India, Mahatma Gandhi, who himself approximated the Indian peasant in his appearance, in his mode of thinking, and in his political imagery, still chose Pandit Nehru, the westernized Indian, as his successor. I don't think that the children of that peasant will believe in the magic of transmuting the stone into God, nor did the painter work on his canvas that way. He sought an objective form, there, on the canvas, for his perceptions and ideas, and he couldn't ignore the experimentations in western painting.

Still why did the painter move me with his argument? Why do we educated Indian writers of my generation—most of whom now belong to the middle-class intelligentsia—suffer from a nagging self-doubt? Why are we all soliloquists and monologuists—the stream of consciousness technique is very popular with our novelists—whereas the older generation of writers, who were also English-educated and belonged to the upper classes and castes in India, did not think that their perceptions were limited to themselves? Perhaps as they belonged to a generation that was involved in the struggle to free India, they felt a common destiny with the masses of India, which in the post-independence India we don't feel. They did think that they wrote and spoke for the whole country, whatever be the quality of their writing, a good deal of which was sloppy, sentimental, and revivalist. I even envy the home-spun plain khadi clothes they wore, which were egalitarian symbols in the post-independence India of Gandhi but which no longer are, because they are the clothes of our corrupt politicians and ministers. We do not think that we can be intensely personal and universal at the same time, a confidence which is important for the creation of great art. As a result we keep reacting rather than creating; we advocate the absurd, or in reaction to it admire the authentic Indian peasant: all of them masks to hide our own uncertainties. In the morass of poverty, disease, and ugliness of India, isn't the westernized Indian inauthentic, and inconsequential, and the traditional peasant an incongruous and helpless victim of centuries of stagnation?

Why did it seem to us that to be authentically Indian we should idealize the simple peasant? We had great Indian writers in the past who had a quarrel with the belief patterns of traditional India. In their search for an authentic mode of existence, twelfth century mystical poets in my language, Basavanna, Allama, and the woman poet Akka, were very impatient with the naïve acquiescence and resignation of the traditional Indian mind. They didn't emulate the peasant, but tried to rouse him into an awareness of his inner potential. The great Indian tradition was not merely spiritual and devotional: we had the materialist Lokayata School, the Sankhya System, and Jainism and Buddhism which were atheistic. It is a tradition of intensely conflicting world views, yet our revivalists prefer to select only one aspect of it. Isn't this debilitating romantic strain in us also due to our obsession with the West?

I shall summarily try to pose the question like this: the continuity of tradition of rural India, as well as the gymnastics of the Indian intellectual which begin and end with him, have remained apart, unrelated. Why is there still no reaching out to each other? Why are we not fully possessed of the vital problems of India? And why don't we have the confidence and desire to affect the thinking of the peasant who, in turn, should become creative as some of them did in the twelfth century in my language? If and when the writers of our country give such immediate responsive attention to our situation, would not we then be less obsessed with the West, and wouldn't much that is happening in the West today seem irrelevant to us? The noble Nehru ran the affairs of the country with his face always turned to the West. What will the post-Nehru generation of writers do? Would Gandhism and Maoism, which have many similarities, create in our countries the situation that necessitates the kind of attention I spoke of? But then, wouldn't our literature become monotonous, burdened with one theme, one purpose, one attitude? As Yeats said:

> Hearts with one purpose alone
> Through summer and winter seem
> Enchanted to a stone
> To trouble the living stream.

2

I should take a more professional look at the problem and clarify issues as they are, rather than lose myself in wild speculation as I did now. Yet I do not regret revealing to you the tenor and trend of our minds in India today. I don't want to pretend that I have still overcome the painter's argument; the peasant does bother me, like Anna Karenina's dream in Tolstoy's novel, and I am worried that the underlying assumption of the literary culture in which I write is potentially capable of making the peasant's mode of existence and thinking irrelevant to me. And a large part of the reality of my country is still him, and he is there in my language whose vigour of expression has been preserved by him.

Between any two literatures there can be roughly three kinds of relations: first, the relation of the master and the slave; second, the relation of equals; third, the relation between a developed country like Europe or America and a developing nation like ours. The example for the first is the way the white men imposed their culture on the blacks in America. Yet no imposition can be completely successful. As in music, in literature too, the minority culture of the blacks may contain the creative nucleus that will influence the literature of the whole country. The interaction between the English and the French literatures illustrates the second kind of relationship. When a French historian writes the history of English literature, it is possible that he sees a French writer at the back of all the important English writers.

The third kind of relationship is more complex than the first two. I use economic categories to describe this relationship rather than terms like East and West, for the thought patterns arising from the division of mankind into East and West are often simplistic. In my own country, as it must be evident from my talk, it results in either imitation or frigid conservatism. Only because I am born an Indian I refuse to think that it is a crime to respond more to Tolstoy or to Shakespeare than, say, to Pampa's epic in my language. I must also be aware when I say this that the novels of Karanth in my language, although they fall short of the world masterpieces I admire, are much more relevant to me in forming my sensibility.

We are a very poor, humiliated nation now, but with a rich and highly sophisticated culture in the past. This creates many psychological complications in our relation to the West. The influence of western literatures may either sharpen our attention to our own reality, or it may take our minds away from what is most relevant to our situation. This is the heart of the problem: how can we have a mature relationship? Is it ever possible to have a mature relationship of equals, when the relationship is one-sided? America wants our Gurus, but will she ever *need* our poets and novelists and respond to them, as we respond to American writers? And even this response is often out of proportion to the real merit of the writers, which is still another problem of uncritical acceptance of received opinions from the West.

One of the Hindi writers brought into the discussion Dr Lohia, a Gandhian Socialist thinker who once described Indian intellectuals as either backward-looking, sideways-looking, or forward-looking. The backward-lookers entertain the illusion that the solution to our problem lies in the revival of our past. (Which aspect of our past? The revivalists are highly selective; they ignore the sceptical and rationalist aspects of our past.) If this is the typical thinking of the conservative upper castes in India, the cosmopolites in India always look sideways. Shall we be like America? Or Russia? Or France? Or Britain? They too speak very emotionally about the ancient glory of India, yet they seek their intellectual motivations from the West. They can get very upset about the American atrocities in Vietnam, but they don't raise a finger against the burning of the huts of the untouchable castes by the landlords of Andhra Pradesh in India. They admire Ginsberg's protest and ungentlemanly ways, yet when one of our earnestly radical legislators removed his chappal to beat the corrupt ministers in the Assembly, they were utterly shocked by his lack of manners. They wear the hippie costume, but the material is imported terylene.

But if we think that the great scientific and cultural progress of the West, with its exploration of space and its undoubted creative energy, is related to the famine and hunger among the illiterate peasants of the rural areas of Gulbarga and Bijapur in my state, and that these two interrelated phenomena are bound to react mutually as our people are roused to consciousness, then we have to become forward-looking; not only the people of the East but those of the West, too. The forward-looking Indian will then have to work for approximation among mankind, which is possible only through a new technology, and a new political and economic order which are again related. For the writer in India who has such a vision, the famine in an Indian village, a new literary experiment in French literature, the science that has caused enormous wealth in one part of the globe and poverty in another, the ancient mystical poetry of Kabir and Basavanna—which he may read wearing western clothes, but which still moves him to the depths—all these coalesce into an immediate contemporary reality. He has to make connections much more than he does now, or much of contemporary western literature which he reads does. As a writer, then, he will have to struggle to embody his vision in a language in which you can write like Blake and not analytically like Russell, and which unlike European languages is still rural.

I am sorry to have slipped into such a high note again. I spoke of the cliché postures of the backward-looking orientalism, and imitative westernization: they are really the same. The great sage of the *Upanishads*, Yajnavalkya, was not an orientalist; he was not bothered about his Indian identity. Imitation either of our own past or of Europe leads to sterility; and attention to the immediate reality is warped. Also, as I have indicated earlier, the Indian orientalist chooses to uphold a highly simplified version of India, the image of India created during our freedom-fighting renaissance, an image again moulded in the Victorian narrow sensibility. Even Mahatma Gandhi was essentially a puritan and lacked the richness and complexity of ancient Indian thought.

In reaction against the orientalists and the westernizers, some of our really intelligent and sophisticated writers have created a new kind of work of art, which, apparently, looks Indian and original. Yet in a very subtle manner these works are also Indian equivalents of western models. The conceptual framework into which the material is organized is western. The material is Indian. The details of life, the myths, the folklore, the legends are all there, but you feel 'Why should I read this after reading Kafka or Camus?' You can't borrow the style or form of these writers without their philosophy, their concept of man; it is not neutral like classical realism. I would say there are some 'mental-frames' today in western literature, born out of certain definitions and concepts of man which dominate the literature of the world, and certainly of India, and this has resulted in a monotony. Therefore the Indian writer looking for a new mode of perception is certainly attracted by the simple peasant who has remained through the centuries impenetrable to the cultures of the conquerors. It is important to know that he exists; our hypersensitive, highly personal nightmares will at least be tempered with the irony of such knowledge.

The question then could be put this way: in India, what should happen to the whole country so that we will be forced out of the grooves that I have been speaking of?

3

I will not attempt an answer to this big question but will try to take another look at what makes these grooves in our cultural situation. Is there a relationship between what the writer creates and the expectations of an ideal reader? What I wish to say now is based on the assumption that the implicit awareness of his potential ideal reader is one of the important factors entering into the writer's creative process, the embodying process of bringing a work into existence in a particular cultural context. Let me see then what has been happening in my language. In the classical period of Kannada literature nearly a thousand years ago, the ideal reader, who belonged to the élite class, forming a very small fraction of the society which could read and write, could presumably read Sanskrit also. Therefore he brought to his reading of Kannada aesthetic expectations formed from his study of Sanskrit. The best of Kannada literature in the past is original within the context of Sanskrit literature. Its departures are important, yet they are departures. No good writer limits himself to the expectations of the reader; he extends it, but within a given context. Even now the literates in my language are hardly thirty per cent, and the discerning ideal reader of our literary works is one whose sensibility is formed by a study of English literature. This is the cultural situation in which we are writing; the peasant at the foot of the hill can't read me. His consciousness may enter my work as an 'object' for others like me to read, which will be very different from what would have been if I were aware in my creative process that he was also my potential reader. The socio-economic process that will make him a potential reader may also make him a man of the sideways-looking middle class like us. Is it possible then to have a different context for writing in a country like India?

Yet there is literature in India which cuts across this framework. There were revolutionary periods in our history which saw important socio-cultural changes brought about by great religious movements. These religious poets worked in the oral tradition, and therefore in the creative process itself they had before them both literate and illiterate people. Thus when the illiterate masses were not mere objects and themes of literary creation, but participants in the act of communication, our regional literature underwent a change not only in theme, but in its aesthetic structure. In an important way, this literature created in the oral tradition, since it was not conditioned by the expectation of the Sanskrit educated literati, becomes most daring and original in its imagery, metaphor, and rhythmic structures. There is a big gap between the language and rhythm of classical literature in Kannada of the twelfth century and the language I use today. But the language and rhythm of the mystical poetry of Basavanna, Akka, and Allama, who are also of the twelfth century, is like the language in which I write today. And these poets were radical in their attitudes too. I must make an important point here; their audience which cut across social barriers was an *immediate* one for them. It was not a mass audience to whose taste they catered. The difference is significant.

I don't foresee such a socio-cultural and religious turmoil challenging us to create outside the defined frameworks of the cultural and literary expectations of our highly limited reading public. The oral tradition is still there in India, but the urge to work in it is not found among our English-educated middle class writers. The expansion of the reading public, whether it is brought about by the present system in India or by the kind of Indian Marxists we have now, will again be through a process of modernization and industrialization—and therefore such a literate mass may not create for the writers a qualitatively different writing situation. What we see of the Marxist progressive writing in India is propagandist, its relation with its audience is hackneyed and unproductive; it is not truly a dialogue in the sense that Paulo Freire uses that word in *Pedagogy of the Oppressed*.

I hope you will appreciate why I can't neatly end this paper. What is the best that a writer who has this awareness can do? Perhaps write for himself. But that is not even ideally possible, I would like to add, and yet . . .

9

RELATIVE REALITIES

Images of Adulthood in Psychoanalysis and the Yogas

SUDHIR KAKAR

To be an adult is to be mature. Yet maturity, apart from its universal biological meaning, has neither identical connotations in the world-views of different cultures nor even consists of a set of simple and easily agreed upon concepts within the same culture. In this paper, I intend to explore the notions of ideal adulthood—psychological maturity—in a circumscribed aspect of the western and Hindu traditions, namely in western psychotherapy (predominantly psychoanalysis) and in the various schools of classical Yoga.

At first glance, such an exploration may seem to be a gratuitous comparison between two different realms of experience, between the scientific and the religious, between the empirical and the ideal. It may also be held that such a circumscribed comparison is of limited usefulness in understanding the notions of adulthood in the two cultures. In the contemporary cultural climate of the West, however, psychotherapy can be (and has been) increasingly seen as a modern successor to religion.[1] The search for personal salvation is being replaced by a search for 'happiness' and 'psychic well-being': the 'health' values of psychotherapy, it seems, are replacing the moral values of traditional religion.

On the other hand, the notions of ideal adulthood in India are not the preserve of a few esoteric, religio-mystical schools and philosophies but are very much an integral part of the Hindu world-image which, like the world-images of other cultures, seeks to give meaning to the individual life cycle and provides a template for the flow of inner and outer experience. In fact, I would maintain that the 'triumph of the therapeutic', which has only now begun in the West, was completed in India long ago and has, since, decisively influenced the Hindu view of the nature of man and the universe.[2]

Adulthood in Psychoanalysis

Although psychoanalysts often stress goallessness as the hallmark of the psychoanalytic technique,[3] psychoanalysis as a body of knowledge on the development and structure of the human psyche has a well defined conception of the goals of psychological maturity even when it concedes that these goals are more to be striven for rather than achieved in any absolute fashion. Depending upon the meta-psychological leanings of the individual psychoanalyst, emphasis may be placed on adulthood within the individual life cycle—the goals of the individual psyche—or on adulthood within a social matrix, that is on the adult's functioning within his social environment. Both these sets of goals develop together; they are in fact intimately inter-woven and any separation between the two, such as the one I make here, is only for the purposes of analysis and description. What is, however, rarely articulated in psychoanalytic writings is the fact that both sets of goals are themselves embedded in what Roy Schaeffer calls a 'vision of reality',[4] a shared image on the nature of man and the world he lives in. Such a vision of reality—composed of certain verifiable facts, acts of speculation and articles of faith—unite groups of human beings in specific cultural consolidations. They necessarily involve looking at inner and outer reality from certain angles while ignoring others and appeals to the 'evidence' by adherents of the one or the other vision rarely lead to a more inclusive, universal vision but only succeed in emphasizing their essential relativity. I shall come back to this later.

In their individual aspect, the psychoanalytic goals of adulthood and psychological maturity are encapsulated in Freud's well-known dictum 'where id was, there shall ego be' or 'to make the unconscious, conscious'. Other writers have elaborated on these terse formulations. The 'healthy' adult (and I equate 'healthy' with the 'moral' and the 'ideal') has the ability to tolerate anxiety without being crippled. He has the capacity to experience pleasure without guilt and can adequately distinguish between his fantasies and the objective reality, irrespective of the reality's painfulness and the intensity of his own needs. He has insight into his conflicts; an acceptance of his strengths and weaknesses, and can use his aggressive energies for achievement, competition and the protection of his rights.[5]

On this broad canvas of healthy adulthood, individual writers have emphasized one or the other detail which they consider central to the picture of adulthood and a *sine qua non* for psychological maturity. Thus Michael Balint speaks of the development of a reliable reality testing which enables the individual to maintain an uninterrupted contact with reality, even under strain;[6] Ernst Kris stresses the achievement of an irreversible insight into one's conflicts;[7] Annie Reich emphasizes the acceptance of one's limitations as the hallmark of an adult[8] while from her particular metapsychological perspective, Melanie Klein talks of a reduction in the two basic (depressive and persecutory) anxieties and the development of a capacity to mourn.[9] I must emphasize that I have confined myself here to the goals of psychological maturity in the classical tradition and have ignored some of the newer departures such as those of Bion and Kohut.

In their *social* aspect, the psychoanalytic ideals of adulthood are condensed in another one of Freud's maxims—to be able to love and work. Elaborated, this would imply that the healthy adult has the capacity for loyal and enduring relationships; can use his or her talents, free from paralysing inhibitions, in productive work and is capable of heterosexual pleasure and potency. Once again, individual analysts may stress one or the other aspect of the adult's functioning in his social environment. Thus Wilhelm Reich subsumes all social aspects of ideal maturity under an overarching concept of 'orgiastic potency'—the ability to have frequent, 'good and satisfactory' orgasms with a loving and beloved partner. As Reich baldly puts it: 'A healthy individual who has enough to eat does not steal. An individual who is sexually happy does not need an inhibiting "morality" or a supernatural religious experience. Basically, life is as simple as that.'[10] More comprehensively, Erikson writes of a development of the capacity for *intimacy*, 'a mutuality of orgasm with a loved partner of the other sex, with whom one is able and willing to share a mutual trust and with whom one is able and willing to regulate the cycles of work, procreation and recreations so as to secure to the offspring too, all the stages of satisfactory development.'[11]

Thus in their interpersonal aspect, the psychoanalytic goals of adulthood shift their focus from the individual adult to an intermeshing of adult lives. With his concept of 'care', arising out of the crisis of generativity versus stagnation in late adulthood, Erikson goes beyond the intermeshing of adults to give meaning to adulthood within the cycle of generations as he proceeds to describe the ideals of adulthood in relation to those who are not yet adult and in relation to society's institutions. 'Care', as described by Erikson, is the unfolding capacity of the adult to 'bring up', guard, preserve (and eventually transcend) all that he has generated, produced or helped to produce in the past.[12] This 'care' extends to the adult's work, his ideas, but above all to the younger generation; it is the essential provision of the support for developing egos.

In reviewing the psychoanalytic notions of adulthood, both in their individual and social aspects, one is struck by the pervasiveness of the humanistic ideals of moderation, control and responsibility— by the preponderance of the Apollonian 'golden mean'. For instance, instinctual activity and passions—except perhaps those of the mind—are certainly not denied but controlled, channelled, postponed or sublimated. As Erikson, in writing of adulthood, says, 'A human being should be potentially able to accomplish a mutuality of genital orgasm, but he should also be so constituted as to bear a certain amount of frustration in the matter without undue regression wherever emotional preference or considerations of duty and loyalty call for it.'[12] The guiding principle of adulthood in psychoanalysis is perhaps best expressed by the Latin hexameter, 'Quidquid agis prudenter agas et respice finem' ('Whatever you do, do it with prudence and consider the consequences'). Even one of the most radical of psychoanalysts and a cult figure for many new forms of psychotherapy, Wilhelm Reich, whose emphasis on the orgasm has become an article of faith with many, does not advocate any wild indiscriminate Dionysian sexuality—the glorification of the instinct without regard for its objects—but looks at promiscuity, homosexuality, perversions, etc. as neurotic and, at most, accords his approval to a kind of serial monogamy.

Images of Adulthood in the Yogas

The prudent adult of psychoanalysis would be a welcome and compatible guest in the Yoga schools of 'liberation', irrespective of whether they focus on the way of knowledge and discrimination (Jnana Yoga), detached work and activity (Karma Yoga), devotion (Bhakti Yoga) or meditation (Raja Yoga). For in their preparatory stages, all schools emphasize the development of certain common adult virtues which do not markedly differ from those possessed by by a healthy adult in the psychoanalytic tradition. Thus Jnana Yoga stresses and expects the development of discrimination (*viveka*), dispassion (*vairagya*), tranquillity (*sama*), restraint (*dama*) and so on. Bhakti Yoga talks of discrimination, freedom from passions (*vimukha*), cheerful acceptance (*anavasada*), absence of manic exuberance (*anuddharsha*). Karma Yoga too stresses a similar constellation of adult virtues in which psychic balance, restraint and freedom from anxiety and passions are the core for the seeker (*sadhak*) of liberation. Similarly, in its first two steps of *yama* and *niyama*, Raja Yoga demands the development of the ethical (as distinct from the moralistic) adult.

While the principal Yoga schools (excepting perhaps Karma Yoga) are relatively more concerned with the development of the individual, the social goals of adulthood have been highlighted in the duties prescribed for the householder (*grihasta*) in the Dharmasastras. Again, both sets of goals—individual and social—must be seen as being complementary and evolving together. In a certain sense, whereas the Yogas are the 'psychology' of man in the Hindu worldview, the Dharmasastras constitute the normative 'sociology'; an ideal model of social relations based on a common vision of the nature of man and the world he lives in.

The adult of the Dharmasastras, consistent with the social focus of these texts, is not an isolated being but an individual embedded in a multiplicity of relationships. He is a partner (to the spouse), a parent to his children (and a child to his parents), and a link in the chain of generations and in the history of the race. The personal requirements for adulthood, implicit in the prescribed duties and symbolized in the rituals specific to this stage, are 'loving' and 'caring'. Loving and caring are of course omnibus words with certain specific meanings in the western tradition. We need to look at their contents and connotations in the Hindu view more closely lest we succumb to the illusion of understanding which the use of familiar concepts in a different context is often apt to give us.

The characteristics of a loving relationship, as reflected in the various *vivaha* (marriage) rituals, are manifold. First of all, the adult is expected to transcend childhood (and childish) attachments and to enter an intimacy in which he is both a separate person and part of a new configuration. As a scholar of Hindu rituals somewhat lyrically expresses it: 'They [the man and the woman] are united like two young plants, which are uprooted from two different pots and are transplanted into a new one.'[14] The theme of separate yet fused identities comes out clearly in the verses that the couple repeats in the marriage ceremonies of *samanjana* (anointment), *panigrahana* (grasping the bride's hand) and *hridyasparsa* (touching the heart): 'This am I, that art thou, that art thou, this am I. The *saman* am I, the *ṛk* thou; the heaven I, the earth thou. Come let us unite';[15] 'I add my breath to thy breath, bones to thy bones, flesh to thy flesh, skin to thy skin',[16] and 'Into my will I take thy heart, thy mind shall dwell in my mind. May Prajapati join thee to me',[17] and so on. In addition, the *vivaha* rituals also emphasize stability, procreation, efforts towards worldly prosperity and the ability to bear sexual frustration as the requirements of married intimacy.

Caring for the children, parents, ancestors, gods and all those who need care, is of course the chief quality of the householder. As the etymology of the word *vivaha* (to support, to sustain) suggests, even the intimacy of marriage is not a goal in itself but a necessary step towards the development of adult care and generativity. Caring gives the householder the central position in the Hindu scheme of the life cycle. 'And in accordance with the precepts of the Vedas, the householder is declared to be superior to all of them; for he supports the other three. As all rivers, both great and small, find a resting place in the ocean, even so men of all orders find protection with the householders,'[18] say the *Laws of Manu*, while Vivekananda writes, 'The householder is the basis, the prop, of whole society. The poor, the weak, and the women and children, who do not work—all live upon the householder. . . . The householder is the centre of life and society. It is a kind of worship for him to acquire and spend wealth nobly; for the householder who struggles to become rich by good means and for good purposes is doing practically the same thing for attainment of salvation as the anchorite does in his cell when he prays.'[19]

In summary, the ideals of the first stage of Hindu adulthood—psychic balance, instinctual restraint, freedom from anxiety, development of the capacities for loving and caring—show a marked convergence with what psychoanalysis has come to regard as the qualities of the healthy adult. Yet in the Hindu view, the healthy adult is only a prelude to the liberated adult. Ideally, adulthood does not stop at prudence but must lead towards liberation. It is in elaboration of the goals of the *liberated* adult that the Yogas sharply diverge from psychoanalysis and psychoanalytically influenced forms of western psychotherapy.

The concerns of the individual in the second stage of Hindu adulthood are radically different from those of the preceding one. This change, as I have shown elsewhere,[20] is dictated by the looming realization of the fact of man's mortality and the approaching end of the life cycle. The essence of this change is an unambivalent emotional, and sometimes even physical, withdrawal from the outside world and a concentration of mental interest on the discovery of the 'real' relationship between the self and the world. As Vivekananda puts it, 'When the human soul draws back from the things of the world and tries to go into deeper things; when man, the spirit, which has somehow become concretized and materialized, understands that he is going to be destroyed and reduced almost to mere matter, and turns his face away from mere matter—then begins renunciation, then begins real spiritual growth.'[21]

The assumption that there is another, higher order of knowledge (*vidya*) illuminating man's essential connection with the world, a knowledge that leads him to liberation and 'beyond nature' and which is radically different from our ordinary, sensory and sensuous knowledge (*avidya*) is of course the *leitmotif* of Hindu culture and speculative philosophy—an object of both fascinated acceptance and derisive rejection. I am, however, not concerned with the truth of this assumption. In any case such matters are inseparable from an individual's vision of reality, legitimized not by evidence but by its being shared by a cultural consolidation. Here I am more concerned with the very real consequences that this belief in the possibility of knowing 'ultimate reality' has for the picture of the ideal adult and the Hindu notions of the goals of adulthood.

Consistent with the prescribed shift of mental interest from 'outside' to 'inside', the different Yoga schools have developed different paths towards the common goal of liberation. In Karma Yoga, there is neither a physical withdrawal nor an overt break with the adult's previous activities and life style. What is demanded of the individual in the second stage of adulthood is a conscious and unremitting effort towards disinterested action, towards cultivating detachment from the fruits of work. Raja Yoga, through such psycho-physiological practices as *pratyahara*, *dharana*, *dhyana* and *samadhi* concentrates on the transformation of the individual's habitual modes of experience. Jnana Yoga frontally assaults the portals of *vidya* through the techniques of *sravanam*, *manana* and meditation on the five great sayings (*mahavakyas*) of the Upanishads. Bhakti Yoga, eschewing the sedate piety enjoined for the neophyte, increasingly demands a different kind of devotion (*para bhakti* as contrasted to the earlier *apara bhakti*), comprising the feelings of utter helplessness and complete dependence on the godhead. And at the end of all these paths stands the liberated man, the *jeevan mukta*.

Let us look at some psychological portraits of the liberated man, culled from representative texts, which make for a substantial change from the 'mystical' and metaphorical language in which the subjective experience of liberation has so often been described. In Jnana Yoga:

> Let the ignorant people of the world perform worldly actions and desire to possess wives, children and wealth. I am full of supreme bliss. For what purpose should I engage in worldly concerns?
> Let those desirous of joy in heaven perform the ordained rituals. I pervade all the worlds. How and wherefore should I undertake such actions? Let those ignorant of the nature of Brahman ('ultimate reality') listen to the teaching of Vedanta philosophy. I have self-knowledge. Why again should I listen to them? Those who are in doubt reflect on the nature of Brahman. I have no doubt, so I do not do so.
> I am associationless, neither the doer nor the enjoyer. I am not concerned with what the past actions make me do, whether in accordance with or against the social or scriptural codes.[22]

In Karma Yoga:

> Whose mind in pains is not disturbed, who is in pleasures void of longing, free from love and fear and wrath, that man is of steadfast thought, the saint.
> Who feels for nothing tender love, who when he finds good or bad, rejoices not, nor hates, firm set is that man's wisdom.[23]

In Bhakti Yoga:

> The highest bhakta has withdrawn all his attention from external things and concentrated it upon the Lord within. When he moves about, it is his legs that take him. His mind is not there. His movement is like the movement of fallen leaf.[24]

And Krishna says:

> Till the pores of the body do not spill over with joy, till the mind does not dissolve, till tears of bliss do not begin to flow and the mind does not dissolve in a flood of devotion, until then there is no possibility of purification for the devotee.[25]

From the foregoing discussion, we see that the Hindu conception of the ideal adult can only be understood within a two-stage theory of adulthood. The first stage marks a completion in the process of individual socialization where instinctual activity is tamed and transformed into mature loving and caring relationships. The second stage of adulthood, on the other hand, requires a process of desocialization—an emotional withdrawal and renunciation of libidinal ties. The focus in this stage shifts to a radically different process which is aimed at transforming individual narcissism (with its roots in the primary narcissism of the infant) into its maturest form—the 'cosmic narcissim' of the liberated man. Whereas the first process is a preparation for life, the second process is a preparation for death. As we saw earlier, in the Hindu view death is the only legitimate concern of the later stage of adulthood. Indifferent to humanist ideals and incompatible with the humanistic framework which has strongly influenced the development of psychoanalysis, the second process is often pejoratively called 'mystical' and its aims labelled as pathological and regressive.

The chasm between the Yogic and the psychoanalytic views on the final goals of adulthood is however not unbridgeable. There is a bridge in Heinz Kohut's concepts of 'mature narcissism', 'cosmic narcissism', and his postulation of separate developmental lines for object ties and narcissistic development.[26] Even closer in spirit (especially to Raja Yoga) is Bion's work. Bion goes beyond the medical model of psychoanalysis and sees the pursuit of O—his sign for ultimate reality represented by such terms as absolute truth, the godhead, the infinite—as the aim of psychcanalytic endeavour. Consequently, he can talk of a stage 'unencumbered by memory, desire and understanding', distinguish between a sensuous and psychic reality (akin to the Hindu distinction between *avidya* and *vidya*) and can write: 'The suspension of memory, desire, understanding, and sense impressions may seem to be impossible without a complete denial of reality; a criticism that applies to what is ordinarily meant by reality does not indicate undesirability for the purpose of achieving contact with psychic reality, namely, the evolved characteristics of O.'[27]

The convergence between psychoanalysis and the Yogas on the meaning of the first stage of adulthood is of course not remarkable, since both deal with human development and its potentials. By the same token the marked difference of opinion on the meaning of the second stage of adulthood—in spite of a few interpretive bridges—should give us pause. Assuming that there is no cultural chauvinism involved—from either side—one of the reasons for this divergence lies in some of the commentaries on the basic Yogic texts and in the pronouncements of many modern Yogis who have hindered efforts at an understanding of the dynamics of the second process and its aims, by gratuitous references to its occult, magical and supernatural nature. Understandably enough, this has turned off many serious students and analysts who have based their evaluation only on this kind of vulgarized evidence. But a more fundamental reason for the divergence in the two images of adulthood lies in the visions of reality that govern psychoanalysis and the Yogas.

The psychoanalytic vision of reality is primarily influenced by a mixture of the tragic and the ironic.[28] It is tragic insofar as it sees human experience pervaded by ambiguities, uncertainties and absurdities where man has little choice but to bear the burden of unanswerable questions, inescapable conflicts and incomprehensible afflictions of fate. Life in this vision is a linear movement in which the past cannot be undone, many wishes remain fated to be unfulfilled and desires ungratified. Fittingly enough, Oedipus, Hamlet and Lear are its heroes. The psychoanalytic vision is however also ironic insofar as it brings a self-depreciating and detached perspective to bear on the tragic: the momentous aspects of tragedy are negated and so many gods are discovered to have clay feet. It tends to foster a reflective adaptation and deliberative acceptance. The tragic vision and its ironic amelioration are aptly condensed in Freud's offer to the sufferer to exchange his unbearable neurotic misery for ordinary human unhappiness. On the other hand, the Yogic (or more broadly, the Hindu) vision of reality is a combination of the tragic and the romantic. Man is still buffeted by fate's vagaries and tragedy is still the warp and woof of life. But instead of ironic acceptance, the Yogic vision offers a romantic quest. The new journey is a search and the seeker (*sadhak*), if he withstands all the perils of the road, will be rewarded by an exaltation beyond his normal human experience. The heroes of this vision are not the Oedipuses and the Hamlets but the Nachiketas and the Meeras.

These different visions of reality, as stressed earlier, combine both the subjective and the objective. Their aim is to impose a meaning on human experience and not, as might be claimed, the discovery of an absolute truth. Inevitably, they set up ideals of psychological maturity and adulthood which may converge in some respects and yet deviate in others. To call such deviations 'pathological'—as some western psychoanalysts are often apt to term the Yogic systems—or to loftily condemn them as 'shallow' and 'based on ignorance of *real* human nature'—as a few Yogis have reacted to the discoveries of psychoanalysis—is to confuse a vision of reality with *the* reality and to remain unaware of the relativity of *all* such efforts which emphasize different aspects of human nature and experience.

Such visions of reality must be understood as pervasively important aspects of psycho-social evolution and, above all, they should be seen in their relative importance for mankind's present position and its radical need for a holistic approach to man's nature. This approach will include and integrate both the unconscious and the conscious, the 'instinctual' and the 'spiritual', the individual and the social, the frailty of man's ego and its strengths, the origins of human development and its goals and values. As a meditative procedure fit for the scientific era, the role of psychoanalysis in this development is crucial. An openness instead of antagonism to other, ancient methods of introspection can but only help psychoanalysis in the evolution of the holistic approach.

NOTES AND REFERENCES

1. See Phillip Rieff, *The Triumph of the Therapeutic: Uses of Faith after Freud,* New York, Harper & Row, 1966; see also Christopher Lasch, 'The Narcissist Society', *New York Review of Books*, 23 (15), 30 September 1976.
2. Sudhir Kakar, *The Inner World: A Psychoanalytic Study of Childhood and Society in India,* Delhi, Oxford University Press, 1978, Chapter II.
3. See 'Symposium on the Evaluation of Therapeutic Results', *International Journal of Psychoanalysis*, 29, 1948, pp. 7–33, and 'Symposia on the Termination of Psychoanalytical Treatment and on the Criteria for the Termination of Analysis', *International Journal of Psychoanalysis*, 31, 1950, pp. 78–80, 179–205.
4. Roy Schaeffer, 'The Psychoanalytic Vision of Reality', *International Journal of Psychoanalysis*, 51, 1970, pp. 279–97.
5. For a summary and discussion of the psychoanalytical goals see Robert S. Wallerstein, 'The Goals of Psychoanalysis: A Survey of Analytic Viewpoints', *Journal of the American Psychoanalytic Association*, 13, 1965, pp. 748–70. See also Stephen K. Firestein, 'Termination of Psychoanalysis of Adults: A Review of the Literature', *Journal of American Psychoanalytic Association*, 22, 1974, pp. 873–94.
6. Michael Balint, 'The Final Goal of Psychoanalytic Treatment', *International Journal of Psychoanalysis*, 7, 1936, pp. 206–16.
7. Ernst Kris, 'On Some Vicissitudes of Insight in Psychoanalysis', *International Journal of Psychoanalysis*, 37, 1956, pp. 445–55.
8. Wallersteir, op. cit., p. 754.

9. Ibid., p. 759.
10. Wilhelm Reich, *The Sexual Revolution*, New York, Pocket Books, 1975.
11. Erik Erikson, *Childhood and Society*, New York, W. W. Norton, 1963, p. 266.
12. Erikson, 'Human Strength and the Cycle of Generations', *Insight and Responsibility*, New York, W. W. Norton, 1969.
13. Erikson, *Childhood and Society*, p. 265.
14. Raj. B. Pandey, *Hindu Samskaras*, Delhi, Motilal Banarsidas, 1969, p. 227.
15. *Gobhila Grihya Sutra*, II. 2.16, in Pandey, op. cit., p. 227.
16. *Paraskara Grihya Sutra*, I. 11. 5, in Pandey, op. cit., p. 228.
17. Ibid., I. 8. 8.; cf. Pandey, p. 227.
18. *The Laws of Manu* (G. Buhler, tr.), *Sacred Books of the East* (M. Müller, ed.), vol. 25, Oxford, Clarendon Press, 1886, pp. 214–15.
19. Vivekananda, *The Yogas and other Works* (S. Nikhilanada, tr.), New York, Ramakrishna–Vivekananda Center, 1953, p. 467.
20. Kakar, op. cit., Chapter II.
21. Vivekananda, op. cit., p. 432.
22. *Pancadasi of Vidyaranya* (Swami Swahananda, tr.), Madras, Ramakrishna Math, 1967, pp. 327–31.
23. *Bhagavadgita*, II. 56–57 (W. D. P. Hill, tr.), London, Oxford University Press, 1931, p. 123.
24. Sadananda Saraswati, *Narada Bhakti Sutras*, Rishikesh, Divine Life Trust Society, 1952, p. 168.
25. *Bhagavata Purana*, XIV. 24. 23–24.
26. See Heinz Kohut, *The Analysis of the Self*, New York, International Universities Press, 1971.
27. W. R. Bion, *Attention and Interpretation*, London, Tavistock Publications, 1970, p. 43.
28. For a detailed discussion see Schaeffer, op. cit.

NOTES ON CONTRIBUTORS

1. U. R. ANANTHA MURTHY, born in 1932, is a Kannada poet and novelist. He is Reader in English, Mysore University and the author of ten books of Kannada poetry and fiction, including *Samskara* (tr. into English by A. K. Ramanujan, Delhi, 1976).

2. VEENA DAS was born in 1945 and is Reader in Sociology, Delhi School of Economics. She is the author of *Structure and Cognition: Aspects of Hindu Caste and Ritual* (Delhi, 1977).

3. ERIK H. ERIKSON, born in 1902, is Emeritus Professor of Human Development, Harvard University. He is the author of *Childhood and Society* (New York, 1950), *Young Man Luther* (New York, 1958), *Insight and Responsibility* (New York, 1964), *Identity: Youth and Crisis* (New York, 1968), *Gandhi's Truth* (New York, 1969), *Dimensions of a New Identity* (New York, 1974), *Life History and the Historical Movement* (New York, 1975) and *Toys and Reasons* (New York, 1977).

4. SUDHIR KAKAR was born in 1938 and is Homi Bhabha Fellow at the Centre for Study of Developing Societies, Delhi. He is the author of *Frederick Taylor: A Study in Personality and Innovation* (Cambridge, Mass., 1970), *Conflict and Choice: Indian Youth in a Changing Society* (Bombay, 1971), *Personality and Authority in Work* (Bombay, 1974), *The Inner World: A Psychoanalytic Study of Childhood and Society in India* (Delhi, 1978) and is the co-editor of *Understanding Organisational Behaviour* (Delhi, 1971).

5. B. K. RAMANUJAM, born in 1929, is Associate Director and Professor of Psychotherapy at the B. M. Institute of Mental Health, Ahmedabad. Besides many papers in professional journals, he has contributed a chapter to *The Indian Family in Change and Challenge of the Seventies* (New Delhi, 1972).

6. SATISH SABERWAL was born in 1932 and is Associate Professor of Sociology at the Centre for Historical Studies, Jawaharlal

Nehru University, New Delhi. He is the author of *The Traditional Political System of the Embu of Central Kenya* (Nairobi, 1970), *Mobile Men: Limits to Social Change in Urban Punjab* (New Delhi, 1976), editor of *Beyond the Village: Sociological Explorations* (Simla, 1972), *Towards a Cultural Policy* (New Delhi, 1975), *Process and Institution in Urban India* (New Delhi, 1977), and co-editor of *Stress and Response in Fieldwork* (New York, 1969) and *Urgent Research in Social Anthropology* (Simla, 1969).

7. Durganand Sinha, born in 1922, is Professor and Head of the Department of Psychology, Allahabad University. He is the author of *Indian Villages in Transition* (New Delhi, 1969), *Motivation of Rural Population in a Developing Country* (New Delhi, 1969), *Academic Achievers and Non-achievers* (Allahabad, 1969), *The Mughal Syndrome: Psychological Study of Intergenerational Differences* (New Delhi, 1972), *Studies in Industrial Psychology* (Agra, 1972) and *Motivational and Rural Development* (Calcutta, 1974).

8. S. K. Thorat was born in 1949. He is a Research Scholar at the Centre for Regional Development, Jawaharlal Nehru University, New Delhi.

INDEX

adolescence, 7, 15; not recognized as a developmental phase in rural India, 37–8, 49; extended, 49

adulthood: *passim*; what it really is, 27; enquiry into nature of, 89; ideal, 118; in psychoanalysis, 119–21; healthy, 119–20; psychological goals of, 120; images of, in yoga, 121–8; Hindu conception of, 123–8

alienation, 47, 110

Ambedkar, B. R., 22, 70, 72, 75, 77, 82, 83, 84, 86

asceticism–eroticism conflict, 100, 102

ashramas (stages of life), 3–4, 6, 15, 101–2

Balint, Michael, 120

Bergman, Ingmar, *Wild Strawberries*, 30–3

Bergson, Henri, 101

Berreman, 66

birth control 29

brahmacharya, 7–8

Chaudhuri, Nirad, C., 58, 61

Child: effect of absent father on, 40; effect of separation from parents, 43–6; super ego of, 50

childhood, 16, 22–3; early, 6; neglected in Hindu system, 15

Chowdhry, Kamla, 13–14

contamination (sex), 95–6

Das, Veena, 19, 21

daughter, 90–4

daughter-in-law–mother-in-law conflict, 48

death, attitude to, 98–9

development: human, 3–4; Hindu

view of, 4; psychological, 17 *et seq*; stages of, 37

dharma, 4–6

D'Souza, Victor, 65

Einstein, A., 14

endurance, individual, 54

Erikson, Erik, 3, 38; his model of human development compared with *ashrama*, 3–4, 6–11, 101; on developmental stages, 37; on identity formation, 37–8, 41; on identity confusion, 39, 57; on identity vacuum, 46–8; on conscience, 50; on sex relations, 52; on youth's confusion of values, 53; on limit of individual endurance, 54; on individual behaviour, 82; on adulthood, 120–1

family, nuclear *v.* joint, 39

Gandhi, Mahatma, 111, 115

garhasthya, 8–9

Gavi, R. S., 71, 79

generativity, 27–8

Gibbon, Edward, 105

girls, treatment of, 26

Goffman, Erving, 96

Guerrero, Leon, 57

Hartmann, Heinz, 3

hero-images, 58–60

'hope', 7, 18

householder, 123

identity: *passim*; stigmatized, of untouchables, 21, 66–75; formation, 24, 26, 37–8, 49, 63–4, 74–5; adjustment, 25; confusion, 39, 57–8, 63; definition of, 66

infancy, 6, 16, 17, 20

Klein, Melanie, 120
Kohut, Heinz, 126
Kris, Ernst, 120

life, stages of, 3–4, 6–10, 26, see also *ashramas*
literatures: and rootlessness, 107; 'insiders' and 'outsiders' in, 107–8
Lohia, Ram Monohar, 114
Lynn, David, B., 40

mass media, 62
maturity, psychological, 118–20
Mencher, Joan, 66
moksha, 4
Murthy, Anantha, *Samskara*, 30,103
Myrdal, Gunnar, 57

Nehru, Jawaharlal, 111

O'Flaherty, Wendy, 102
old age, 9; privileges of, 100–1
Omvedt, Gail, 83
orientalism, backward-looking, 115

play-age, 22–3
pollution, 21
Premchand, *Godan*, 102–3
psychotherapy, 118

Rama Reddy's *Samskara*, 30–4
Ramanujam, 25–6
Reich, Annie, 120
Reich, Wilhelm, 120, 121
'ritualization', 18–19, 21, 26–7

role as mask, 97
role-models, 58–9, 62–3

Samskara, 30–4
Sarabhai, Mrinalini, 14
Sarabhai, Vikram, 13, 14, 34
Satyashodhak Samaj, 83, 84
Schaeffer, Roy, 119
scheduled castes, 65 *et seq*
Schlesinger, Ben, 39
school-age, 22–3
self-image, deflation of, 47
semen, 99
sex relations, 52–3, 99–100
Shakespeare's seven ages, 15–16
Sobti, Krishna, 92, 94, 95
sons, treatment of, 26, 90
sterility, 96
super-ego development, 61

Temple, R. C., 94, 95, 97
Tilak, B. G., 83

wife–mother conflict, 99–100

vanaprastha, 8–9
Vivekananda: on householder, 123; on renunciation, 124

widowhood, 97–8
Wild Strawberries, 30–3

youth, 27, 57; and parental guidance, 51–2; revolt of, 53; response of, to socio-moral dilemma, 60–2; and mass media, 62; and identity formation, 62–4